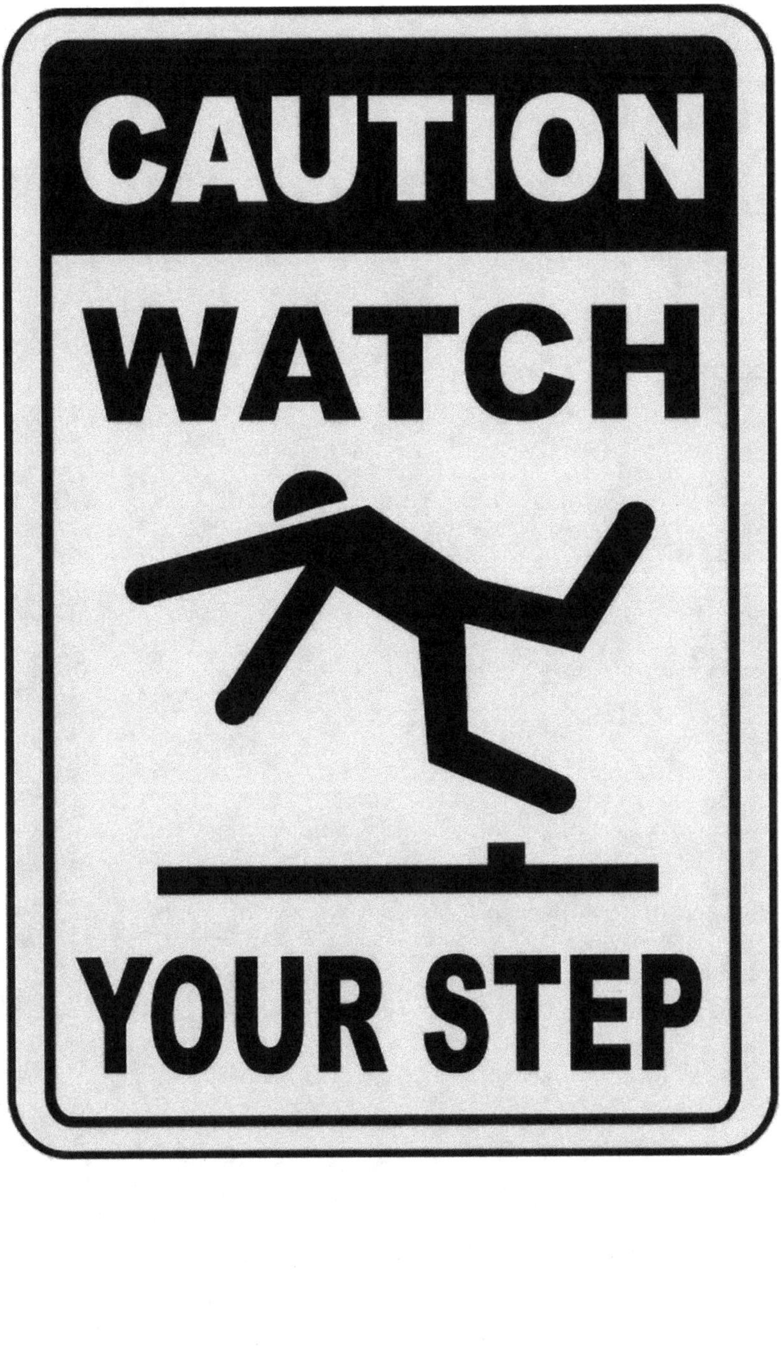
CAUTION
WATCH
YOUR STEP

Martìnì Alley

and other swashbuckling adventures of a certified Klutz

ALSO BY DIANE KLUTZ

Round Eyes: An American Nurse in Vietnam
You Can't Sleep Here

Martìnì Alley

and other swashbuckling adventures of a certified Klutz

DIANE KLUTZ

Illustrations by
JONATHAN BROWN

Georgetown, Texas

Martini Alley
and Other Swashbuckling
Adventures of a Certified Klutz
Copyright © 2022 by Diane L. Klutz

All rights reserved.

Printed in the United States of America.

No part of this book may be reproduced in any form without written permission from the author except in the case of brief quotations embodied in critical articles and reviews.

Cover and book text designer
James Retherford/Hot Digital Dog Design

Illustrator
Jonathan Brown/ Inkstains.com

First Edition

Library of Congress Cataloging-in-Publication Data application is pending.

ISBN: Paperback: 978-1-7379739-0-4
ISBN: Kindle E-reader: 978-1-7379739-1-1

204 Hobby St.
Georgetown, TX 78633

DEDICATION

This book is dedicated
to Jim and Cindy Spalding
for patiently enduring the Klutzes
for over fifty years.

You're our heroes and best buddies.

CONTENTS

Foreword
Acknowledgements
Part One *Becoming a Klutz* — 1
   What Is a Klutz? Definitions — 2
   1 *Welcome to the World of Klutz* — 3
   2 *How I Became a Klutz* — `5
   3 *Skinny-dipping in the Officer's Club Pool* — 13
   4 *Klutz Rides to the Rescue* — 22
Part Two *Home Wasn't Built in a Day* — 31
   5 *Dream House on Nightmare Mountain* — 32
   6 *This Old House* — 40
   7 *Los Tres Amigos* — 47
Part Three *The Saga of* Martini Alley — 53
   8 *Have Tattoo, Will Sail* — 54
   9 *Romancing the Waves* — 63
   10 *The Birth of* Martini Alley — 71
   11 The-Boat-With-No-Name — 75
   12 *The Return of* Martini Alley — 80
   13 Martini Alley: *The Final Voyage* — 84
   14 *Revenge of* Martini Alley — 95
   15 *Farewell to* Martini Alley — 102
   16 *The Mystery of the Phantom Slasher* — 105
   17 *No Good Deed Goes Unpunished* — 109

Part Four *Happy Hour With the Sea Gods*	113
18 *Klutz Dives Into the Drink*	114
19 *Paradise Lost-and-Found*	124
Part Five *Land Yachting*	133
20 *Hot Wheels*	134
21 *The Birth of Big Bertha*	142
Part Six *Epilogue: Where Next?*	159
22 *Sailing Into the Sunset*	160
About the Author	168

FOREWORD

The saga of *Martini Alley* began as an email attachment that I sent to family and friends shortly after Stephen and I returned home from the buoy disaster. I expected some sort of reaction, either disbelief, laughter, or both, from a few recipients; but was totally blown away by the sheer number of positive responses. Those who had sailed or motor-cruised said they connected immediately to the story. My uncle, a retired Navy captain, said he had experienced every mishap described, just not on one trip. The others simply enjoyed the read.

Following that initial incident came more boating calamities and naturally more writing. The first more formal renditions of *"Martini Alley"* and "Revenge of *Martini Alley*" appeared in the *Island Moon*, a Port Aransas, Texas, newspaper. Several years later, they were featured in a Georgetown, Texas, magazine called *Sun Rays*. I had so many requests afterwards from folks who wanted to hear more that I gathered my old handwritten notes and started typing—umm, word processing.

Even though many of the adventures started as

journal entries, the rest were recreated from chatting with friends, photos, and so forth. Memory lane strolls were a limitless source of information, but not dependable or entertaining enough for the tale I wanted to tell.

Hence I followed Mark Twain's advice, "Never let the truth mess up a good story."

Hopefully, it worked, and you enjoy reading these stories as much as I did when writing them. And for that ...

I thank you.

ACKNOWLEDGEMENTS

Getting this book to completion was such a group effort that I hardly know where to start in expressing my gratitude, but I will give it my best shot.

First, I am eternally grateful to Stephen, my husband, for allowing me to poke fun at his expense and for always encouraging me. Without you, sweetie, there would be no *Martini Alley*.

To Shannon, my beautiful daughter, thank you for the millions of suggestions and your never-ending support.

Thanks also to Joan, Linda, Cindy, Susan, Merry, Teri, and Marge who provided needed feedback while graciously reading and re-reading chapters. Your input and encouragement were invaluable.

A huge thank you to the Lady Puckers, my shuffleboard team at Wriggley's Pub. You are the best cheering squad ever.

Unending gratitude to John D. Moulton, author, artist, my website designer and, most of all, the person I bounced ideas off throughout this project. I am also grateful to John's wife, D'Ann, for putting up with my many phone calls.

Thanks to my dear friend, art director, and editor James Retherford at Hot Digital Dog Design for his wit, creativity, and for sticking with me all these years. Even when I got cranky, he never gave up.

I am also grateful for the generosity of Jonathan Brown, cartoonist *extraordinaire*. Thank you for believing in my project and being a part of it.

Lastly I want to acknowledge my family, friends and even a few strangers for encouraging me to finish this book. I had many stops along the way, but you guys kept me going.

MARTINI ALLEY

and other swashbuckling adventures of a certified Klutz

PART ONE

Becoming a Klutz

DEFINITIONS

What Is a Klutz?

Klutz: noun, slang.

n. Slang
1. A clumsy person.
2. A stupid person; a dolt.
3. A fool, lout, or boor.

[Yiddish klots, from Middle High German kloz, *block*, *lump* from Old High German.]

klutz'i·ness *n.*
klutz'y *adj.*

American Heritage® Dictionary of the English Language, Fifth Edition.

ONE

Welcome to the World of Klutz

Call me Klutz.

No, seriously. That's my name—Klutz.

I was not born a Klutz. As a child I was not prone to tripping, falling (except on ice skates), or dropping things. No broken bones, even after falling from a tree. When I was perhaps four or five years old, I did, however, split open my chin, which resulted in stitches. And I cut my back crawling under a barbed wire fence.

Other than that, my life was klutz free—that is, until I married a Klutz. He was not one of the popular *Klutz Bird* Klutzes or the Klutz book series of whatever Klutzes, or even the famed *Mad Adventures of Captain Klutz* by Don Martin.

My Klutz was a tall, handsome army lieutenant who just happened to jump out of airplanes and do other adventurous feats. He also had the surname of Klutz. But I didn't consider his name odd. I knew a lot of people with strange last names. For instance, Mumper, my maiden name, was considered strange by many people. Therefore, a guy named Klutz didn't faze me a bit.

It's hard to imagine now, but in the late sixties' klutz was not a word frequently heard outside the Yiddish-speaking communities of Brooklyn, at least I'd never heard of it.

If someone dropped something, he or she was just clumsy. If someone tripped, a remark about having two left feet was normally used.

But to call someone a klutz? Now that was something I'd never heard of until I officially became one—a Klutz, that is. I swear the moment I said, "I do," I did. Fall, trip, slip—you name it; I did it all.

I even walked face first into a glass wall at the University of Texas at Arlington, gashing my leg, nearly breaking my nose, and suffering severe humiliation as a billion pieces of non-tempered glass fell around and on me.

To make matters worse, the doctor who stitched up my leg was laughing so hard about me being a Nurse Klutz that he forgot to numb the area. I also think he wasn't concentrating fully because the next day the stitches ripped out. Forty-nine-plus years later I still have a nice round scar to prove I am the real thing.

And now as I endeavor to keep my two left feet out of my mouth and firmly planted on the ground, I will forge ahead ...

... to the story.

TWO

How I Became a Klutz

First a little background about how, when and where Klutz and I met.

Fort Gordon, called Camp Gordon until 1956, is a post located near Augusta, Georgia. Built in 1941, Camp Gordon became the headquarters for three infantry divisions during WWII. During that war it also served as an internment camp for German and Italian prisoners of war as well as the disciplinary barracks for convicted Army criminals. After WWII, it became a separating service center for Army personnel.

In 1948, Camp Gordon acquired two major military schools: the Military Police School and the Signal Corps Training Center. During the Vietnam War, Fort Gordon expanded to include basic training and advanced individual troop training. Camp Crockett, located within Fort Gordon and established in 1967, served as the preparatory training site for the Advanced Airborne Infantry until 1969.

Many soldiers, including my husband, Stephen, aka Klutz, received their introduction to military life at Fort

Gordon. From basic through Airborne and then Signal training, he and many others survived the heat and humidity as well as the physical, mental, and emotional demands supplied freely by the U.S. Army.

Suffice it to say, Fort Gordon was and still is a place steeped in rich military history and honor. This was especially true during the Vietnam War. The commanding officers took pride in keeping the rank and file in order, mandating proper uniform and decorum. Always! After all, this was why they were senior officers: to give orders and demand to be followed.

In a perfect military world, this worked. But during the final years of the Vietnam War, not so much. Fresh from duty in Southeast Asia, thousands of junior officers swarmed military posts, including Fort Gordon. Their mission? Have fun and raise hell until their military commitment was completed. Their motto: "I'm short [i.e., soon to be discharged] and I've already been to Vietnam."

Now enter Klutz and I into the picture.

It was early afternoon in late May 1971 when I arrived at the BOQ (Bachelor Officers' Quarters) at Fort Gordon after returning from a six-month tour in Vietnam. I was dressed in a proper Army summer uniform: Green cord skirt and jacket, dark green hat, stockings, and black leather pumps. Due to the Georgia humidity, I was sweating profusely, and my hair, once tucked up under my hat, was hanging limply on my shoulders. A definite no-no.

Lugging a Samsonite suitcase past my stack of boxes, I pulled the door handle towards me just as someone pushed it open from the inside, nearly knocking me backward over my stack of stuff. It was a man.

My withering glare did not go unnoticed, as he apologetically drawled, "Sorry." Grabbing my arm to keep me from falling, he added, "Ya moving in or just visiting?"

I thought it was an awfully stupid question, given that I was surrounded by boxes and suitcases, but I decided to answer anyway. "Moving in," I said, tilting my head up so that I could see his face.

"Well then, welcome," he proclaimed loudly as he pumped my hand. "My name is Stephen Klutz, but everyone calls me Steve or Klutz." Continuing without pausing for a breath, he asked, "What room y'all in?"

I looked around to see if another person was standing behind me. Finding no one else, I concluded that "y'all" could mean any number of people. I didn't ask for clarification; I just told him the room number.

A huge Cheshire cat grin spread across his tanned face, highlighting his white teeth. "Well, I'll be damned. You're right across the hall from me."

I wasn't sure if this was one of those good news/bad news type of things, but before I had a chance to ponder the thought, Stephen—aka Steve or Klutz—grabbed my suitcases and my hand and led me down the hall to my room.

I unlocked and opened the door and gazed inside. The hooch that I shared with my roommate Ginny back in Vietnam was furnished with only a bunkbed and two desks with chairs, a hotplate, a small dorm-size refrigerator, and a scrounged-up crate and two stools to complete the ensemble.

In comparison, this BOQ room had a real bed, a two-burner stove/oven combo, a normal-sized refrigerator with freezer, a desk with chair, and a small dinette with two chairs. The best part was a full bathroom: tub and shower and as much hot water as I wanted. It was a mansion, and I was in paradise.

Brief introductions were followed by emptying the car of boxes. And then Klutz—that's what I decided he should be called—insisted he was now taking me on a tour of the four story BOQ. No amount of arguing swayed him from his mission and so I gave in, plodding behind as we climbed to the top floor. I tried focusing on what he said, but mostly he just rambled. Soon my mind started drifting off to random thoughts such as "where the hell is this guy from, anyway," and "what do I do about supper."

Before I could dwell on these topics long, we completed the upper floors and were back on the ground floor. We moved past our rooms to the entry foyer where on the left was a retail dry cleaning/laundry establishment. A display of enthusiasm on my part was probably appropriate at this point, but I was so exhausted from the car trip and the forced guided tour that all I could do was to mumble, "Convenient."

The effervescent Klutz didn't seem to notice as he abruptly stopped in front of a pair of barred glass doors.

"And this," he said almost triumphantly as he spread his arms towards the doors, "is the bar. Can you believe we have our own bar?"

"**With pool tables!?!**"

This more-statement-than-question sounded like a proud father showing off his long-awaited son instead of a young man showing off a drinking establishment. I had to admit that, despite my increasingly foul mood, I was impressed with all the amenities. Seriously, this place was better than many upscale apartment complexes in D.C. I would have been more impressed, however, if the bar actually had been open. But it wasn't, and at that point I didn't care. I just wanted to escape to my room.

I hadn't seen other females in the BOQ, and that made me curious. But due to getting settled in and dealing with work assignments, I didn't have much opportunity to ask around.

It was now Saturday and time for me to discover the laundry facilities up close and personal. With dirty clothes loaded in my arms, I trudged to the second floor and pushed open the laundry room door. Only instead of swinging inward, it swung back, nearly toppling me over. Grabbing my falling clothes, I looked up. Standing in the doorway was a woman holding a laundry basket of what appeared to be clean clothes.

Excited to at last meet another female in the building, I hurriedly introduced myself, and she did likewise. She was a captain in the Women's Army Corp, her room was on the second floor, and for the last three months she had been the only female housed in the BOQ.

"What?" I exclaimed, my jaw nearly scraping the floor. I couldn't believe that there were only two females in the entire building. I knew many of the nurses I worked with lived off-post, but what about all the other female officers? Where did they live?

I started to question the captain further, but she was already heading back to her room. As she opened her door, she stopped, turned, and said something that didn't make any sense.

"Be-careful-what-you-wash!?!"

Those five words bounced around in my head as I separated whites and darks into appropriate piles. Carefully putting my new silky bras, undies, and baby-doll pajamas into one washer and my everyday clothes into another, I walked down to my room. Thirty minutes later, I returned, hanging my lovely lingerie on the drying rack and putting the rest of the clothes in the dryer.

Going back to the first floor, I saw that Klutz's door was open, and he was talking on the phone. As I turned to go to my room, he yelled, "Diane, come here and talk to my mother!"

I turned back. He was standing in the middle of his room holding the receiver out to me.

"You want me to do what?!?" I hollered back. "I don't know your mother. I barely know you."

"Doesn't matter. She just wants to say hi."

I reluctantly took the proffered receiver, said hi and a few other niceties, and then handed the phone back.

That was weird, I thought. Who would do that?

Klutz said a little more to his mother and then hung up.

"Where ya from?" he abruptly asked.

"Pennsylvania," I replied. "In the country outside of Pittsburgh, close to West Virginia. You?"

He seemed to stand straighter as he said, "Arlington."

"Oh, a home boy," I said. "I've been to Virginia a bunch of times. I was stationed at Walter Reed before I went to Vietnam."

"Virginia?" he asked incredulously. "No, Texas!"

I had never heard of Arlington, Texas. The only Arlington I knew about was in Virginia. And I told him as much.

His mouth fell open as he stared at me like I was stupid or something. "Uh, you know, Six Flags Over Texas... between Dallas and Fort Worth?"

"Nope, never heard of it."

I could play this dumb game too. And with that I left him and his Arlington and returned to the laundry room. After emptying the dryer, I reached over to grab my undies from the rack. Only there were no undies! The rack was empty. I frantically searched all the dryers, washers, every place. Nothing!

Then I ran downstairs, yelling along the way.

"What the hell are you hollering about?" Klutz shouted as I burst into his room.

"My clothes are gone." I blubbered, wiping away tears while trying to explain what happened.

Klutz just stood there, staring incredulously at me. After almost a minute of silence, he said, "Someone stole your clothes?"

"Didn't you hear what I just said?" I was now shouting. "Someone stole my underpants and bras."

The surprised look on his face quickly morphed into mirth. "You mean you left your underwear up in the laundry room? In plain sight?!? Are you crazy!?! Of course, your underwear and stuff are gone. There are fifty men living here, and most of them have just returned from war."

Trying to control his amusement—but failing—he handed me a wad of toilet paper indicating that my nose was dripping big time.

Blowing into the tissue, I asked, "Why would men want my underwear? What would they do with them?"

Like Mount Vesuvius, Klutz erupted into gales of laughter. Tears rolled down his face as I stared at him.

"You really are naïve," he said, trying to catch his breath. "Men do stuff like that."

I wanted to slap that laugh off his face, but instead I shook my head glumly. "Well, unless they were messed up, they wouldn't wear them, and surely they wouldn't give them to a girlfriend or anything. They're used!!!"

Klutz was choking from laughing so hard, but I didn't care. I turned my back to him, slammed the door, and stomped back to my apartment.

At least now I understood what the captain meant when she told me to be careful about what I washed.

I just wish she would have been a little more specific.

THREE

Skinny-Dipping in the Officers' Club Pool

The Annex Bar at the Fort Gordon's Bachelor Officers' Quarters was a favorite place not just for us young officers, but older, seasoned officers as well. For instance, there were these three (full-bird) colonels who showed up at precisely three o'clock every afternoon and sat on the same three chairs at the far side of the bar facing the entrance.

They always drank straight vodka, commiserated with each other about the sad state of the current military, regaled anyone who would listen with tales from their glory days, and ogled the young female officers. When sitting upright became an issue, they would stumble to their respective cars and drive home, often followed closely by an MP.

The truth is most folks who visited this and other bars on post became casualties of the fifty-cent martinis, manhattans, and grasshoppers (along with other concoctions), including sloe gin fizzes. Thankfully, when we overindulged at the Annex, most of us just had to crawl down the hall to get home.

One Friday evening about a month after I moved in, Klutz and several of his buddies were entertaining themselves at the pool table when I, along with four of my nursing friends, arrived at the bar. The guys joined us at a table and settled in for some serious drinking.

After a few pints, Klutz announced that he had a plan. I always loved a man with a plan, so I listened up. He said in downtown Augusta there was a dance club called the Partridge Inn. According to Klutz, it was a favorite hangout for military and civilians alike—famous for its bands, booze, and dance floor. The idea of going to a dance club was so irresistible, so filled with thoughts of drinking and dancing, that we piled into two cars and headed towards oblivion.

I was not disappointed. The Partridge Inn was absolutely perfect—cheap booze and a large dance floor. Thousands of miles away, the war was forgotten as songs such as "Jeremiah Was a Bullfrog" (aka "Joy to the World"), "We Gotta Get Out of This Place," and "Proud Mary" blasted through the speakers. Life was once again wonderful.

We were the last ones standing—or sort of—when the music stopped, and the manager kicked us out. Even though it was two in the morning, we were not quite done with having fun.

Reluctantly we piled into our cars and headed back to the BOQ. As we staggered into the building, looking more than a little worse for wear, two of the guys started bickering over what to do next. Klutz, not one to stay quiet for long, chimed in, "Let's go skinny-dipping in the Officers' Club pool!"

Stunned silence fell over the group. "Uh, I don't think that's a good idea," one of the guys said.

One of the girls added, "We will really get into trouble if we get caught."

Like tipsy bobbleheads, everyone nodded.

"Oh, come on." Klutz groaned. "Don't be party poopers. We won't get caught. Besides, Major McCoy, the man in charge of the Officers' Club, and I are buds. Let's go. It will be fun!"

Seeing no response, Klutz finished with a rousing challenge, "I dare you! In fact, I double-dog dare you."

It might be because I was raised with three brothers, but I never ever turned down a dare, let alone a double-dog dare. So I straightened to my full five feet three and a half inches and declared, "That's it. I'm in! Now who's coming with us?"

No bobbleheads in sight. Our fellow officers appeared more like the spinning heads in *The Exorcist*.

I looked around at the blank faces in front of me, but only Klutz was smiling—or rather smirking—like a cat who had just caught the canary.

"I guess I'm the canary," I thought.

It was close to three o'clock in the morning, and Steppenwolf's "Born to Be Wild" was blaring through the car's speakers as we pulled into the dark parking lot outside the Officers' Club. Stars were visible in the night sky, despite the humidity-thickened air that made breathing difficult. Or perhaps that was just me having a panic attack.

Klutz emerged from the car first. As I crept out of the passenger door, I stared at the ten-foot-high fence surrounding the pool area. The gate was shut and bolted.

"Oh, how sad," I said, with just a smidgen of sarcasm mixed with relief. "We can't get in, so I guess the bet's off!"

Instead of acknowledging the obvious and returning to the driver's seat, Klutz simply turned and stared at me. "Are you kidding?" he asked, seemingly astonished that I would even consider such a thing. "We just climb over the fence."

And with that he was up and over.

The fact that Klutz was an Airborne-trained Green Beret never crossed my mind as I muttered, "Well, if he can do it, I can too."

I put the toes of my shoes into the spaces of the chain link fence and started to ascend. Descending was a little trickier, but with Klutz's gallant aid, I landed with a plunk and an audible "oomph" on the hard concrete. A quick inventory later I was pleasantly surprised to find that my bones, ligaments, and joints were intact. Klutz and I stood silently facing the blackness of the swimming pool.

"Let's do this," Klutz quickly said, shucking his clothes and piling them into a heap. This was followed by a loud splash. I looked up to see his head above the water. "Come on in. It's warm."

Yeah, right, I thought. I told him to turn around and while watching him to make sure he wasn't peeking, I proceeded to take off my dress, hose, slip, and bra. But undies? No way was I taking them off after losing six pairs to the panty thief. No way!

Gritting my teeth, I tentatively stepped into the pool's dark depths, not quite trusting in Klutz's proclamation of its tepid temperature.

I was right. Not only was the water *not* warm, it was downright frigid. Goosebumps popped up on top of goosebumps. Cuss words spewed from my mouth.

And ... then ... I stopped ... and listened.

At first I wasn't sure, but after a minute I knew. It was the faint sound of a siren from a police car or ambulance. The wail grew louder and closer, until there could be no doubt that it was heading towards the Officers' Club ...

... and us.

Bright headlights, accompanied by whirling red and blue lights, careened into the parking lot. I ducked my head under the water, hoping to escape notice, but I was out of luck.

A booming command, "Stand up and turn around," reverberated through the water to my ears. Like an alligator peering from the depths, I peeked towards the source of the command and saw two military police standing in front of their vehicle, hands resting menacingly on their holsters.

Klutz abruptly stood, holding his hands up over his head and looking very much like Peter Sellers' Inspector

Clouseau in *The Pink Panther.* In a voice attempting to command as much dignity as possible, he said, "It's okay, gentlemen. I am Lieutenant Klutz, and my—*ahem*—companion is Lieutenant Mumper. I am a friend of Major McCoy, the commanding officer in charge of the Officers' Club. I have his permission to swim here whenever I want."

He forgot to mention that he didn't have permission to break into or climb over the locked fence, but at that point I wasn't going to correct him.

Acting like he had not heard a single word that Klutz said, the biggest of the MP duo bellowed, "Sir, get out of the pool. Now!"

No one could accuse Klutz of not following orders, so without further ado he quickly exited the water, buck naked and dripping as he walked over to his pile of clothes and proceeded to dress. He tried drying off with his shirt, but when a deep growl erupted from one of the MPs, he gave up that idea and just pulled on his clothes. Too bad we didn't think to bring towels.

Meanwhile, still in the water, I remained in my alligator pose, not moving a muscle.

"Ma'am," the shorter MP barked in my direction. "You must get out of the pool, too."

I knew from my nearly two years of military life that MPs were trained to be watchful and to carefully observe and study details in each situation they encountered in the line of duty. This situation was no different. As I peeked in their direction, I noted a turn of their heads as they looked over at my heap of clothes on their side of the pool and then at me on the other. I couldn't see them in the darkness, but I could imagine their eager anticipation at the prospect of watching a young blond naked lady officer scramble out of the pool in the middle of the night.

Hoping to quell their excitement, I stood up in waist-deep water with my arms crossed over my chest, thanking my ancestral gene pool that I was not overly endowed. I sounded more courageous than I felt as I yelled back, "I will not leave this pool until you both take your hands off your gun holsters and turn around. You can also turn off the car's spotlights."

I thought I heard a low chuckle, but surprisingly the MPs did as I asked. And I did as they asked—got out of the water, that is.

By the time we were fully dressed, the MPs had unlocked the gate and were waiting beside their vehicle. Without a word, we scrambled into Klutz's car and left the premises with the police close enough behind to make sure that we really were leaving. No blaring music this time.

I couldn't look at Klutz as we drove back to the BOQ. I was mortified, especially when imagining what the police report would say about our escapade. We were going to be in so much trouble.

Like most of us newly returned from the war, I was impervious to the rules and regulations of Army existence. I muttered with a bravado I didn't feel, "So what can they possibly do to us? Send us to Vietnam? Been there, done that."

To which Klutz sarcastically replied, "Ever hear of court martial?"

I immediately shut up.

Next morning—or rather later that morning—I went to work with the dreaded expectation of being called to the company commander's office at any moment. My head pounded from the effects of too much alcohol, too little sleep, and fear of the unknown. Instead ... nothing. Not a peep ... from anyone.

Finishing my shift, I went to the BOQ Annex in search of Klutz. As usual, he was at the bar sitting next to the three birds, having a seemingly grand time.

I headed toward him, but before I could open my mouth, he grinned in his Cheshire Cat way and said, "Everything's okay. In fact, the major laughed so hard reading the report that he could hardly speak. He finally gave me a 'sort-of' reprimand and told me never to do that again. Or at least not get caught."

I was dumbfounded. "What about me?" I asked.

"It seems your name was not mentioned in the report. There was a reference to a young blond female being in the pool with me, but nothing specific. You're off the hook."

My joy at being not busted, however, was short-lived. Since nothing stays secret on an Army post for very long, rumors involving us, the officers' pool, and the MPs abounded, growing more scandalous with each telling.

By the end of the day, not only had Klutz and I been caught skinny dipping, we had also been nabbed breaking into the bar to steal gin, hot-wiring a jeep and riding naked across the firing range, and any number of other assorted misdeeds.

Perhaps, given enough time, all of that might have happened. However, we could only lay claim to the original transgression.

FOUR

Klutz Rides to the Rescue

I'd like to say that getting caught skinny-dipping by the MPs was the night Klutz and I fell in love—but I won't, because we didn't. We hardly spoke to each other after the skinny-dipping experience.

My friends thought I was embarrassed by the whole incident and was simply avoiding him. But that wasn't it. I just didn't want to get involved in a serious relationship. It didn't matter anyway because Klutz was so busy entertaining "waiting wives" at the Main Officers' Club that he didn't have time for me.

Waiting wives were the wives who were waiting for their high-ranking officer-husbands to return from Vietnam or some other deployment. By creating a special group, deployed officers' wives were able to socialize in a sanctioned setting without compromising their marriages and/or their husbands' careers. Or so the thinking went.

Most nights the wives congregated at the Officers' Club to drink, dance, drink some more, and flirt with the junior officers. Rumor had it that occasionally these activities extended beyond the club, but for the most part no hanky-panky was involved. Probably because many absentee colonels or generals assigned one of their junior officers to escort the wife at the club, just to make sure. At least that's the explanation Klutz gave me.

Sounded rather weird to me.

What eventually did bring Klutz and me together was a barroom brawl in a place called the Bottoms. It was a genuine redneck dive bar and pool hall located on the Georgia-Florida line and notorious for beer, loose women, back-room high-stakes pool games, and knock-down-drag-out fights. It was also off-limits to military personnel. But that didn't stop Klutz and his buddies from going there from time to time.

On several occasions I asked Klutz to take me, but he always refused. He said it was no place for a girl like me, and I would only get in trouble if I went.

Not about to be deterred, I asked an army reservist whom I occasionally dated to take me. Since he had not heard about it, he agreed.

Growing up near Wheeling, West Virginia, didn't prepare me for the scene in front of me as we entered the bar. It was like a dilapidated saloon in a cowboy movie, minus the grizzled old piano player and the trapeze-swinging girl. Despite the sawdust and piles of peanut shells, my shoes stuck to the floor as I worked my way to the bar.

Surveying the surroundings, my date looked skeptical. "I'm not sure this is a good idea," he said.

With more bravado than I felt, I said, "Oh, it's okay. Just looks scary. Let's get a beer."

So my date and I grabbed a couple of beers and headed to an empty booth, shoes still sticking. The place was so filthy that I hesitated to sit down for fear of what could come crawling under my feet and up my legs. Vietnam had not prepared me for this.

Before I had a chance to take a swig of beer, I saw Klutz entering the bar through a closed door on the far side of the room. I smiled and waved, but he didn't smile back. In fact, he looked pissed. About what I had no clue, but when I saw him stomping over to our table, I figured it wasn't good.

Without glancing at my date, he grabbed my arm and dragged me through another door to a path leading to the river far below.

"What the hell do you think you're doing?" he yelled above the still-blaring music. His brown eyes glared at me. "Don't you know how dangerous this place is? It's off-limits. By the way, how did you get here?"

Before I had a chance to point out that he too was hanging out at the same dangerous off-limits dive, he turned and stormed back into the joint. I followed close behind him—probably a little too close behind him because when he stopped abruptly, I smacked into his back with a loud "Oomph."

Acting like he didn't know me, Klutz looked around the room several times. Finally he turned to me and said, "So where is he? You know, your so-called date."

That comment was not called for, but I decided it was best to ignore it. I then scanned the area too, but no luck. Apparently the clientele in the bar was too rough for his taste, and so my "so-called date"—who was also my ride back to the BOQ—had made a quick exit.

"Great," I mumbled. "Now how do I get home?"

Klutz grabbed my arm, but this time he took me to a booth, plunked my beer on the table, and growled with his best Lee Marvin voice:

"STAY HERE UNTIL I COME BACK!!!"

And with that he stomped into the back pool room. Being curious, and also not one to follow orders, I waited until the door closed and then snuck in behind him. The room was huge—at least twenty pool tables. Beer bottles, money, and cigarettes were scattered everywhere.

I spotted Klutz at one of the tables just as the sound of breaking glass and loud cussing exploded around me. Bar stools clattered to the floor as men jumped into action. A guy not far from me went down as a flying beer bottle hit his head. Instruments of harm appeared from nowhere as I stood there—literally stuck to the floor.

And that, my dear readers, was when it happened. Klutz, my hero, appeared at my side. He wrapped one of his arms around my waist, and brandishing a knife in his other hand—looking *very* Errol Flynn—he hauled me through the melee. His friend followed—only instead of a knife, he had a gun.

Once outside, Klutz plopped me down on the gravel drive and told me to run. And run I did and, for once in my life, without asking questions. The three of us made it safely to the car and with screeching and spinning tires escaped back to Fort Gordon.

A month later, just before he left active duty to return to the Arlington in Texas, Klutz proposed. To my surprise, I accepted.

I say "surprise" because Klutz was nothing like the man I thought I would marry. Like most girls, I thought I would end up with someone like my father—quiet, unassuming, agreeable, and even-tempered. Klutz was none of these. He was vivacious, outspoken, loud, and always the life of the party. He was fun, and I had fun being with him. Our lives would never be boring.

Back on the home front—my parent's home, that is—I had to tell my folks about marrying Klutz. When I left for Vietnam, I was seeing a guy whom my mom really liked, and the vision of the two of us getting married was dancing in her head. The fact that he was taking a military leave to get his PhD from Harvard didn't hurt his marriageability standing with my mother either. She nagged me constantly about marrying a doctor, and even if a PhD was not a "real doctor," it was close enough.

But six months in South Vietnam changed me, and I no longer wanted the same things as I did before, including Harvard man. With considerable trepidation, I prepared to face my mom.

Unfortunately she got the jump on me. "Well," she said before I could set down my suitcase, "How's Rob?"

"Uh, I guess he's fine. Probably still at Harvard." I said, thinking this was a good way to lead into the subject. It was not.

Her voice rose several octaves as her smiling face contorted into anger. "What? You didn't break up with him, did you?"

"Uh," I mumbled once again, unable to think of anything else to say. "Yeah, I did."

Mom's five-foot-two-inch stature immediately gained five more inches as she glared at me, tears threatening.

"Why?" she demanded as the dam holding her tears broke, flooding her now reddened face. "Your cousins are married. What's wrong with you? Nobody's good enough for you. Is that it?"

As quickly as the torrent started, it stopped as her deflated body sank onto the kitchen chair. "You're never going to get married, and I'm never going to be the Mother of the Bride."

So that's the problem, I thought. Four of mom's sisters had married off their age-eligible daughters, except her. I was the lone hold-out. At the ripe-old age of twenty-two, I was on the brink of becoming a lost cause.

"Mom," I said gently. "That's what I came to tell you. I met a guy, and we are getting married."

Her body bolted upright out of the chair as the blazing fire of hope ignited under her. "Really?" she sputtered, madly wiping the traces of tears from her face. "This is wonderful news. Go tell your father."

I don't think she even asked what his name was, let

alone anything else about him. She was finally going to be the Mother of the Bride.

Three months later, Klutz and I were married in my family's church in Taylorstown, Pennsylvania, and I became, in the eyes of the United States Army, Lieutenant Mumper-Klutz. The wedding announcement in the local paper simply read, "Diane Mumper Marries Man from Texas."

Strange as that announcement was, it ranked a mere five out of ten on the strange announcement scale, compared to the one printed thirty years earlier when Klutz's folks got married.

His mom's maiden name was Clapp, which was enough to elicit smirks and giggles, but when she married Klutz's dad, who was a cadet at Texas A&M University, the Cadet Corp announced in the university paper, **"Klutz gets Clapp on Night of Matrimony."**

And that, dear readers, was just the beginning. Stay tuned for more.

and other swashbuckling adventures of a certified Klutz

MARTINI ALLEY

and other swashbuckling adventures of a certified Klutz

PART TWO

Home Wasn't Built in a Day

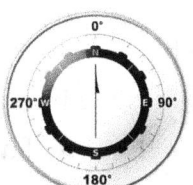

FIVE

Dream House on Nightmare Mountain

Now officially hitched, we visualized doing what newlyweds do. Not *that*. This is the PG version.

No, we would venture forth, discover our dream house, and transform it into a forever home—a shelter against the storm. At least, that was what most folks would have done.

Being Klutzes, however, meant that we did nothing like most folks. From the get-go, I knew that living with Klutz was not going to be easy—exciting, interesting, unconventional, yes—but not easy. He had the ability to weave the worst idea possible into an illusion that it was the best. And I always fell for it. The skinny-dipping episode was just one example.

Finding a forever home was no different. It became our own quixotic quest for Nirvana. And like Don Quixote, our quest was always out there, somewhere yet to be found. We would find it or die trying.

Our quest had also been our challenge, and Klutz and I never stepped away from a challenge—whether on the land, on the sea, or in the sea.

Forget planning. Also forget patience, especially when I'm involved. I single-mindedly attack everything with equal determination.

My favorite sayings
Right, wrong, or indifferent, just make a decision!
Poop or get off the pot!
I'm not getting any older!
and as Admiral David Farragut said at the 1864 Battle of Mobile Bay:
Damn the torpedoes, full speed ahead.

After fifty years of marital bliss, nothing has changed. Except our houses, which we've changed more often than the weather in Texas in March. In fact, during those fifty years, we'd moved at least twenty-six times and to four different states—but mostly in Texas. I averaged it out, and as of this writing we've changed living places every 1.92 years. I am not sure whether that is a Guinness record or not—but it could be.

Moving frequently was arduous to say the least, but at least we get rid of a lot of clutter. That and I never worried about spring cleaning—just packed it up and cleaned the house when empty. **Done!**

One of our Denton, Texas, friends (who also moved frequently) once told me she figured changing homes was a lot cheaper than changing husbands. I'm not sure I agree with that because for the amount of money spent on packing paraphernalia, paying the moving companies, and time and effort involved, Klutz and I could have divorced several times over.

Come to think of it, we came pretty darn close once or twice.

I would not consider us experts in home ownership, unless you count the number of homes owned and lived in. However, of the twenty-six different living abodes, only seven have been in house or apartment rentals. That means we've purchased nineteen—twenty if I include the house we bought in Colorado and sold the day after closing without ever living in it.

The simple part, in my opinion, was the getting or the getting rid of a house. The nearly impossible part was finding one that was both perfect and affordable. That's where the Colorado story begins.

We'd been renting a house in Englewood, Colorado, for two years while trying to find our dream home. Our girls were in elementary school, and we wanted to be away from the city, but the prices were beyond our reach. So we decided to buy a lot in the country and just build one.

We found the perfect site: an acre lot situated on the edge of Pike's National Forest in a place called Perry Park, northwest of Colorado Springs.

The fact that we had never actually built a house didn't deter us one bit. We had the land. Now all we needed was a plan. Being daring to the point of stupidity, we shunned advice to get an architect and found what we wanted from *Better Homes and Gardens*. A modified A-frame, perfect for mountain living.

With sheets of blueprints in hand, we were armed and ready. There was one itty-bitty problem ... we didn't have a builder or contractor.

A friend from church named Mickey stepped up to the plate and said he had "some experience" in home construction as a subcontractor. Because he was currently "between jobs," he could start "right away." We hired him on the spot.

Sadly Mother Nature had different plans—frozen ground. Perry Park was 6,500 feet in elevation at its base. Since our lot was much higher, it was well into June before the ground thawed enough for digging to begin.

In addition, there was the issue of a roadway—or lack thereof. A narrow trail connected our lot to the main road.

The county was no help. However, they said that, if we built the road, they would maintain it. This sounded like a good plan—until we discovered that in order to create said road, we would have to dig through red clay and rocks. The county got the better end of that arrangement.

Then, of course, we needed permits for the water well and septic system as well as for gas lines and site plan approval. Half of our house budget was spent before we even got started.

Construction finally got underway. Mickey located a great crew, and by mid-August our new home was framed and ready to be closed in. Shingles, roofing material, and cedar boards for the exterior were delivered. Sheetrock lay in stacks along with our windows, and we had the best tasting cold water, thanks to the efforts of the driller.

But then came September—and, with it, calamity. Our crew left. Without warning, they just packed up and fled to lower ground. Maybe with winter around the corner, they didn't want to get snowbound in the mountains. Too bad they didn't share that tidbit of information before they signed on.

Mickey remained optimistic. "We can do this."

Klutz and I looked at each other and then back to Mickey. "We!?! We both have full time jobs!"

He retorted, "Do you want to get this house built?"

At this point in the story, I need to backtrack several months. The Klutz family four (plus two dogs and a hamster) had to vacate our rental house and were staying in my parents' twenty-four-foot trailer, parked at a KOA campground south of Castle Rock next to a major freight train track.

The first night in the trailer was an experience equal to Dorothy and her tornado. At two in the morning, the trailer started to shake and shudder, building quickly to tremors of earthquake magnitude. Anything not secured inside a cabinet crashed onto the floor. These convulsions were punctuated by the rapidly repeating horn blast from an oncoming freight train—and it was headed right at us!

We huddled together, our hands over our ears, certain that at any moment the oncoming train would crush the little camper like a tin can. Gradually, however, the blaring and rumbling decreased and receded into the distance, and before long all was peace and quiet, as if nothing had ever happened.

Every night thereafter, at exactly two in the morning, the southbound freight train made its thunderous way past our tiny camper, and we learned not to dive for cover when we heard its approach. After a week, we hardly noticed it at all.

Needless to say, by September we were more than ready to complete our house and move in. Even though the main construction crew was gone, at least we still had electrical and plumbing subcontractors working. We were on our own to do the rest—walls, roof, sheetrock, flooring, insulation, windows, and hundreds of other major and minor jobs.

The first task was the roof. Its steep 65-degree pitch required professional roofers who cross-trained as mountain-climbers, but the professionals had headed for warmer climes. In retrospect, of course, building a roof with that degree of slope was not a great idea, but at the time we had no intention of building the roof by ourselves.

Being taller, sturdier, and more limber, Klutz took on the task of placing and nailing the shingles, while the shorter, stockier Mickey carried them up the ladder. I had the job of securing the support beams to the house frame with hurricane clips. I think I only smashed my thumb a few times, but the folks in the neighboring valley would know for sure.

Klutz, however, was not so lucky. Like Mickey and I he suffered bruises, cuts, and sundry injuries, but it was his fall off the roof, as recorded in the official "Klutz History of Hard Knocks," that nearly did him in.

The "unofficial" version confirms that he rolled off the roof, but thanks to airborne training and a pile of loose shingles to cushion his landing, there was no permanent damage—except to his ego.

The first snow arrived on schedule, and, like most first snows, it didn't remain long on the ground. It was enough, however, to remind us that more was coming, and we had better get the house ready.

As in days of old, we called on our church friends to help. And help they did. From the oldest to the youngest, they pitched in.

I was in charge of the sheetrock crew, Mickey supervised the taping and bedding process, and Klutz took on the windows and outdoor decking.

Fortunately for us, a few of our volunteers were engineers—and not the train types. Even if I say so myself, when all was said and done, we had the straightest, most perfectly plumbed decks and sheetrock in the history of all house building.

And the house was exactly as we pictured it ... perfect. We loved living in the mountains. Large outcroppings of red rocks became snow slides for the girls. Ice skating on the golf course ponds was a daily winter activity, as was cross-country skiing. During the warmer months, we hiked the many trails and river beds. We had found our Shangri-La.

However, the powers-that-be weren't about to let us get comfortable in our paradise. In 1986, oil prices plummeted, and with it so did Klutz's oil business. We had to sell and move back to Texas.

As difficult as it was, none of us regretted the decision to build that house. We learned a lot—sheetrocking, taping and floating seams, and laying shingles, but more importantly the value of friends.

But the most valuable thing we learned was never to build a house alone.

Hire a reliable contractor and crew.

SIX

This Old House

Have you ever dreamed of finding a really cool old home in a historic area to remodel?

We did ... and we did.

Fast forward to June, 2001. We were living in a beautiful custom home in Denton, Texas, at the time, but after five years—a record for us—we got the itch. We didn't just want to move; we wanted to go all Bob Vila and sink our teeth into a truly "This Old House" project.

Klutz called me at work one day. "Meet me today on Parkway Street. Found us a house. Ad is in the paper."

The ad should have been my first clue of the potholes lurking ahead.

> **Cute fixer-upper near the heart of Historic Denton, just two blocks from downtown.**
> **Divided into three rental units.**
> **Must see to believe.**

First of all, the phrase "fixer-upper" should have scared us off. It didn't. And when we saw the house?

A North Texas EF-5 tornado couldn't compare to how quickly we were sucked in.

Our rose-colored glasses firmly in place, we toured the home that we just knew would put us in *Southern Living* magazine. Original wood floors were in many of the rooms, a claw-foot tub adorned one of the bathrooms, and stained French doors with glass knobs separated the two main sections of the house. There were also two other baths—*sort of.* There was one *real* kitchen in the largest unit, but only a dorm fridge, microwave, and hot-plate in the other two.

All of this at an amazingly low price!

Never mind that the wood floor was so worn that we couldn't tell what color it had once been ... or that the shower in one bathroom was just a tube sticking out of the wall ... or that the claw tub was painted purple on the outside and rusted on the inside.

All we saw was a diamond in the raw, just waiting to be transformed into a rare gem.

The best part was the history of the place. According to the tax records, the house had been built in three separate stages. The 1925 original was a kit house, either Sears or Montgomery Ward. A 1926 addition next to the original was the mirror opposite of the first, with matching porticos in front and on each side. The rear addition, dated 1930, appeared to be an afterthought; it was not built on pier and beam like the rest of the house but on beams laid directly on the ground. It could have been used as a storage shed, rather than living quarters.

Another interesting aspect of the home was that the original family took in boarders, which was a common practice during this period. The newly created Girls Industrial College (renamed Texas Woman's University in 1957) beckoned young women, and since dormitories were unacceptable living quarters for proper ladies, other arrangements were necessary. Offering room and board provided a safe atmosphere for these young women as well as extra income for the homeowner.

Thoroughly enthralled by these findings, we signed the contract and put our house on the market. It sold immediately, and within two weeks we were packed and ready to start our new adventure in remodeling.

We had just one teeny-weeny glitch.

We had nowhere to go.

Our original idea was to move into the most livable side of the house while remodeling the rest. On closer inspection, though, we came to the conclusion that this was impossible. There was no "livable side."

For one thing, the floors tilted so much that when a ball bearing was dropped at one end, it rolled downhill to the other, picking up speed as it went. The bathroom shower (the one with the pipe sticking straight out from the wall) had no water, but that was probably for the best. And the kitchen? Trust me, you don't want me to describe the dozens of health hazards lurking in every nook and cranny.

So Klutz and I, along with our two dogs and one cat, moved into a top-floor one-bedroom apartment.

Why the top floor?

Klutz wanted the top floor because he didn't want to hear tromping sounds over our heads. He failed to consider trekking up two flights of stairs with groceries or the three-to-four-times-a-day-and-night canine potty breaks.

Back at the Parkway House, Klutz started demolishing walls. It didn't take long for him to realize he was up to his armpits in alligators. One afternoon while he was sitting forlornly on a bucket, staring at the mess surrounding him, a tall, thin hippy-looking man walked in and looked around without saying a word.

Klutz looked up at the man and after a few bewildered minutes asked, "Can I help you?"

"No," responded the man in a quiet voice. "But I think I can help you."

Thoroughly baffled at this point, Klutz stood and introduced himself. The man presented himself as Kurt and said that he and his wife lived in the house behind ours. He then said something that caused Klutz's jaw to hit the floor: Kurt was an experienced house remodeler! What's more, he was not currently employed and would be *interested* in helping us. But only if Klutz *needed* him.

NEED HIM?!? Klutz was downright exuberant. He grabbed Kurt and hugged him like a long lost brother. Then he handed him a beer and said, "Let's get to work."

That day a beautiful friendship between Kurt and Klutz was formed. Not only was Kurt a blessing, he was a marvel to behold. He could move a doorway from one part of a wall to another. He found oak flooring that matched ours, ripped out the two kitchenettes to create closets, and found the best plumbers and electricians in Denton. Maybe not the best, but they were the cheapest. He was fun, always cheerful, and a hard worker ... when he showed up.

You see, Kurt really was a hippy—a genuine relic from the Sixties. According to his many friends, he dropped a little too much acid during his youth in the exclusive Highland Parks area of Dallas. As a result, his brain did not always fire on all cylinders. He no longer took hard drugs or even drank alcohol. But he loved his marijuana.

Work progressed as smoothly as possible, and six months later we were ready to move into the main side of the house. There was just one little problem—or rather one big problem.

No toilet.

There was a hole in the floor—just nothing on top of it. Kurt had been tasked with obtaining a toilet, but as the movers were unloading our stuff, he was MIA. Of course, I panicked.

Five hours later Kurt nonchalantly walked in, cradling a commode in his arms. "Sorry," he said as he studied the boxes and furniture. "Are you moving in today?"

I sighed.

The other half of the house was more complicated than we imagined. The add-on room at the rear was a nightmare. The wood flooring, under the flea-infested rug, was rotten. The only thing we could do was rip it up and toss it out, but until we could get a foundation contractor to set pier and beams, we were left with a dirt floor. I felt like Laura in *Little House on the Prairie.*

Undaunted, Kurt set up plank walkways so that we could move around and placed our ficus tree named Fred in the middle of the dirt floor.

"Fred now has a home," he proudly stated. It was rather fitting for the circumstances.

Spring rains arrived early, and soon water was flowing like a river under our feet and around Fred. Klutz and I would wake to the sound of storms and rush to our "mud room" to get the sump pump going, while also using buckets, along with lots of cuss words, to bail the rising water.

In spite of all the setbacks, working on a house that old was fun, especially when something unexpected was discovered. For example, while working on the main kitchen, we discovered the walls were not hollow, as they were in the rest of the house. Instead they were shiplap wood, buried under layers of discolored newspaper and old wallpaper.

There must have been a kitchen fire sometime in the past, because when we removed the last layer of wallpaper behind the stove, the shiplap was charred.

The best surprise, though, was uncovering a large brick chimney in the kitchen where the pipe from a wood stove had once been vented.

The not-so-fun part was the nonstop projects that constantly needed attention. There was no AC, except for a wall insert in our bedroom, and the only heat source came from outdated ceramic gas wall units, which would definitely not pass any building codes. From rethreading the window pulleys to sanding and repainting all surfaces because of the high probability of lead-based paint, the list went on and on.

At least Kurt now had a steady source of income.

Fourteen months after we started, the major renovation of the Parkway House was complete. Or mostly complete. The mud in the mud room had sprouted into a gigantic walk-in closet. The claw tub was refinished, boasting turn-of-the-last century hardware, and sat in a magnificent master bathroom with pale green paint and white-beaded wainscoting.

The back sitting room was surrounded by double French doors opening to the back yard, the old wood floors had been polished, period hardware installed on all the doors, and lace curtains hung on the lower half of the large windows. We even installed sixteen-inch black and white linoleum squares in a checkerboard pattern on the kitchen floor.

But after nearly two years, it was time to move on. Our "old house" was bought by friends, and twenty years later they still live there.

Better than that, they love it.

SEVEN

Los Tres Amigos

Our next foray into the building and remodeling business came two houses and four years later. I was teaching in the College of Nursing at Texas A&M University in Corpus Christi, Texas. We rented a spectacular town house, but within a year we wanted to buy our own place on one of the boat canals that crisscross the north end of Padre Island.

Since canal homes were insanely expensive, we focused on interior ones. We eventually found an affordable house which was across the road from a large canal and had a backyard perfect for a swimming pool. Klutz and I obviously suffered from acute memory loss about the minefield that is remodeling. Because despite needing work—lots of work—we bought it.

First on the agenda, find a pool contractor. Next find a painter and a handyman.

At this point I must offer a word of advice: never-ever listen to someone who says he knows a good, affordable handyman who can do anything from painting to flooring to complete remodeling. Especially if this handyman lives on the Texas-Mexico border and only requires up-front gas money and a place to stay while working.

This jack-of-all-trade's name was Gonzo. Seriously. I'm not making that up. Lured by the idea of inexpensive labor, Klutz called him, and, sure enough, he said he could do the flooring and whatever else was necessary. Moreover, he was more than happy to travel from the border to Corpus Christi if we provided him a place to stay.

I checked around, and even the cheap motor inns on the island cost more than our budget allowed.

I suggested we buy a tent so he could camp out on the beach like other folks, but Klutz didn't think that was a good plan. After much heated debate, I agreed that he could stay in the house until it was ready for us to move in.

Several days later, Gonzo arrived—with two other men. "Hey," he said in broken English. "They will help so I can finish faster. And you don't have to pay them as much as me."

As if he read my mind—or saw the expression on my face—he continued, "No worry. Jesse is minister. He is sponsor for Joe who just got out of jail. Drugs. But we go to AA meetings. All is good. We take care of house. No drinking. No *problema*."

If that was meant to reassure me, it didn't.

Klutz responded to my concerns with the Good Samaritan argument, "We have to give folks a chance, and what better chance than by having them do an honest day's work."

Chiding myself for being uncharitable, I gave in.

"You can live here," I said. "But here are the ground rules: no smoking in the house, buy your own food, keep the bathroom cleaned up, no renting movies from cable, go to AA meetings daily, and yada yada yada." I sounded like my mother.

Surprisingly, the boys appeared to be behaving and were on the job by eight in the morning. That was the *first* week.

The second week Klutz had to physically shake Jesse and Joe awake at ten. You can guess where this story is heading—right into the crapper.

The three hombres were no longer attending AA, as evidenced by the liquor and beer bottles scattered throughout the house. Cigarette butts littered the back patio, and porn movie billing popped up on our cable account. I discovered this last tidbit when the cable bill came in at $400.00. Gonzo blamed Jesse, the preacher man.

"I don't care," I shouted. "They have to go."

Klutz suggested a compromise. "What if we let Gonzo stay and finish, but preacher man and his sidekick go south?"

That sounded great ... *except* they had no transportation and no money ... *because* they had spent it all on cigarettes, booze, and porn. So we forked over the dinero for two one-way bus tickets to Matamoros, Mexico, and Jesse and Joe were gone.

A week or so later, Klutz realized that Gonzo also needed to be gone. The guy's work was substandard. The ceramic tile flooring he installed was a mess, the master closet walls he constructed were crooked, and that was just the beginning of the list.

By now, his truck no longer worked, and since he sent his paychecks to his wife—or so he said—he had no money to fix it. At least that was his story.

Klutz's face hardened, "I am not going to give that man cash to fix his truck. Nor am I going to pay someone to fix it. I'm done being taken advantage of."

Solution? Klutz decided that to avoid a permanent live-in, he would drive Gonzo back to the border with his truck in tow.

And that was adios to the three amigos.

Klutz and I, for once in our lives, decided to eschew drama and just fix the place up ourselves—with the help of some professionals who weren't inexpensive, but they got the job done.

But we weren't finished. The same quest that led us from one building and remodeling adventure to another reared its restless head once again.

Only this time, it led us to water and *Martini Alley*.

and other swashbuckling adventures of a certified Klutz

MARTINI ALLEY

and other swashbuckling adventures of a certified Klutz

PART THREE

The Saga of Martini Alley

EIGHT

Have Tattoo, Will Sail

I have often wondered why humans—not living on or near water—yearn to be on or near water. Perhaps it's a reverse Darwinian sort of thing: our primal urge to return to whence we came. Or a Freudian return-to-the-womb desire.

Whatever the reason, in our mid-fifties Klutz and I felt the urge to cast anchor. We wanted adventure, and what could be more adventurous than sailing? Just thinking about riding the waves of the Seven Seas, basking in the sun on never-ending water, and sipping toddies at sunset made me giddy.

But before I regale you with this tale of high seas adventure, I must ask a question.

What's a sailor without a tattoo?

And my answer is—naked, for one thing.

Probably sober for another.

Seriously, sailors and tattoos go together like peanut butter and jelly or ham and cheese.

I was neither sober nor naked, but I still didn't have a tattoo. Klutz did, however. He and a group of his buddies, all around eighteen or nineteen years old, were hanging out in Fort Worth, Texas, in a rather inebriated state of mind when one of them came up with the bright idea of getting tattoos.

"Hey, great plan," Klutz shouted. "But where?"

As if on cue, a bright neon sign across the street began flashing, beckoning them to "Sailor Bob's Tattoo Parlor."

Like moths enticed to a flame, they stumbled into the shop where, amidst lots of bantering about what type of design each should get, they queued up. There was one rule: the tattoo had to be placed in a visible spot, not on a private area.

Slaps on the back accompanied by whoops of approval greeted each guy as they exited the "chair" with his new body art on display. The guys quickly discovered, however, that the art of tattooing was not a quick process, and by the time Klutz, who was last in line, made it to the "chair," he was practically sober. The thrill of a tattoo was wearing off, and all Klutz wanted was a nap—or at least more alcohol.

With his buddies goading, he surrendered to the needle, and after twenty minutes or so he emerged with the initials SB (his first and middle name initials) on the inner part of his lower right leg. By today's standards, it would hardly be classified as a tattoo, but he was happy.

His mother? Not so much.

My tattoo experience was a little different, mainly because I was on the cusp of turning fifty before I even considered getting one. Up to that point, I was dead set against the idea of injecting dye under my skin.

Both of our daughters had tattoos, which didn't please me at all. Yet there was something bold, even rebellious, about getting "inked" because nurses were expected to be above that sort of display of personal expression. Heck, even fingernail polish was frowned upon unless it was pink or clear.

I weighed the pros and cons of a tattoo but hadn't made up my mind until one beautiful, hot afternoon when Klutz and I were sipping toddies on the beach at North Padre Island. I abruptly jumped up and announced, "I've decided to get a tattoo. Does it hurt?"

Always the go-to-guy for details, Klutz replied, "Nope. Not after the first stick."

Then he asked, "What do you want to get. And where?"

Now those were very good questions, to which I had no answer. I shrugged, "I'll figure it out when I get there. Let's go." A voice in the back of my brain added, "Before I change my mind."

We changed clothes, jumped into the car, and headed to the mainland. Klutz figured that the best chance of finding a suitable establishment or two would be near the Naval Air Station.

He was right. There were at least twenty tattoo shops lining the street like a gauntlet of pain in flashing neon leading up to the main gate. There was Sailor Bill's, Sailor John's, Sailor Jack's, and, of course, a Sailor Bob's, along with a plethora of other names prefixed with "Sailor."

With the help of the *Yellow Pages*, I narrowed the search by ruling out those establishments that were cash-only or were open twenty-four-hours-a-day. My acceptable shops included those that described sterilization procedures, individual ink and needles, and so forth. I excluded all shops that had "Sailor" in its name.

Lilly's Tattoos & Piercing fit the bill. It was next to several eating establishments, had a respectable storefront appearance, and was free of sidewalk trash. So far, so good.

A tinkling brass bell announced our entrance. I surveyed the room in wonderment. It was nothing like I expected. Instead of dark, dingy, and dirty, it was bright, cheerful, and clean. The walls were painted a soft yellow, and the décor was bohemian-like—colorful beaded curtains hanging in the doorways, huge beanbags in lieu of chairs, and incense wafting a smoky trail throughout the room. A Turkish hookah or two would have completed the scene.

Lining the perimeter of the room, several large glass showcases encroached on the calm atmosphere. Klutz strolled over to inspect.

"What the ... !!!" he exclaimed loudly, shattering the serenity within the room. "Diane, come look at this stuff."

Inside the showcases were metal objects, obviously jewelry for body piercing but looking more like medieval torture devices. On display were rings, rods, chains, studs of all sizes, and other items that were beyond my ability to imagine where they could be attached to the human anatomy. The only thing missing was a dungeon with an "iron maiden" and a "rack."

Feeling unnerved by these instruments of agony, I turned to Klutz. The phrase, "Maybe this isn't such a good idea," was hardly out of my mouth when a tall, bearded man parted the dangling beads and approached us.

"G'day to ya. Me name's Tommy. How can I help ya?" he asked in an obvious Australian accent. Dressed in white from neck to toes, he looked more like an old-fashioned surgeon or butcher than a hippy tattoo artist. Not that I've any experience with hippy tattoo artists, but it just struck me as odd and rather scary.

The sleeves on his t-shirt were rolled up to reveal biceps larger than my thighs—which says a lot right there—and were covered in intricately detailed, riotously colored skin art featuring dragons and snakes intertwining down his arms to his fingers.

Klutz and I were mesmerized, and we probably stared longer than was polite.

I tore my eyes away from Tommy's arms and toward his face. "Hi. My name's Diane, and I would like to get a tattoo."

There, I said it. Tommy gave me a crooked smile and asked, "Do ya know what ya want, and where ya want to put it?"

I glanced at Klutz. He shrugged and said, "Don't look at me. This is your thing."

"Fine," I said. "I would like a butterfly, but not too big, and placed on the outside of my right ankle."

Tommy pointed to a bookcase near the grouping of bean bags. "Pictures are there. Pick one out, and I'll go and get the room ready."

I searched through shelves of photo books until I found the one with butterfly art. There sure were a lot to choose from. Evidently butterflies were popular skin designs.

Choice made, I gathered my courage, parted the beaded curtain, and entered surprisingly familiar surroundings. Unlike the bohemian waiting room, this space was set up like an operating room—stark white walls, steel counters, and an examination-type table with a large moveable light suspended from the ceiling. The nurse part of me was reassured, and I nodded my head appreciatively as I said to no one in particular, "At least this room looks better."

The patient part of me—waiting for torture by needles—wasn't as comforted. I just wanted it to be over and done. Klutz sat on a chair next to the table and continued a running commentary about something or other, while Tommy arranged the instruments on the right. He then began to scrub my leg where I wanted the butterfly.

At long last he was organized, and he asked me, "Are ya ready?"

Before I could say "Yes," I felt a sharp stab piercing my ankle.

"**OH SHIT!!!**" I screamed. "That hurts like hell!"

Klutz, whose hand I held in a death grip, calmly responded. "Don't worry. You'll get numb to the pain."

"Sorry, mate," Tommy interjected. "Not true. Every needle is going to hurt just like the first. That and ya have not much skin on yer ankle. Close to bone, ya know, so pain's worse."

With that, another needle pierced my skin, followed by me yelling again—only louder.

Klutz stood to leave.

"Where the hell do you think you're going?!?" I yelled.

"Oh, I saw a liquor store around the corner. I was going to get you a drink. You know, something alcoholic."

"Please," I begged. "Hurry!"

"Sorry, mate," Tommy declared without a hint of compassion. "No alcohol on premises."

Klutz shrugged and said, "Okay. I'll just go out and get something for me and drink it in the car. I'll be back in a few."

If it weren't for Tommy's vice hold on my ankle, I would have bolted upright. "Like hell you will. You'll stay right here until the bitter end. Me no drink, you no drink."

And so the next thirty minutes continued with the needle piercing skin accompanied by my yelling and cussing. Hopefully there was no one close by.

After what seemed like an eternity, Tommy announced that my tattoo was done, and I was allowed to look. There, on my ankle, was this bloody image of what might be called a butterfly. The expression on my face must have given away my dismay because he took a gauze sponge and dabbed some more blood. If I squinted, I could make out a little color, but mostly it was simply red.

Helping me off the table, Tommy reassured me. "This is normal. Ya will be bloddy, but no be much. And it won't be pretty for a bit, but just do what I tell ya on the paper and ya will be fine."

With that he handed me a sheet of instructions and then excited via the beaded curtain to the waiting room and the cash register. I was so grateful I was still alive that I don't remember how much it cost, or even paying for it.

"I'm proud of you," Klutz announced as we walked to the car. "You really did it. I figured you'd chicken out."

"O ye of little faith," I responded. "Now I need a martini or two. Maybe three!"

Ten years later, as I approached my sixth decade of life, I decided I wanted another tattoo. I mentioned it to Klutz, who responded with:

"Are you sure? Remember the last one?"

How could I forget? But much like childbirth, the pain associated with the process was worth the effort whenever I looked at my pretty butterfly. "I don't want to get anything big, just something different. Maybe like a symbol or Zodiac sign."

Klutz thought for a moment and then said, "I want one too. Let's get them identical?"

I wasn't sold on the twinsy thing, so I said, "How's about doing symbols or something unique?"

Klutz looked doubtful about that idea until I showed him several that I found searching the wonderful world of the web.

Agreeing on a Chinese something-or-other symbol, we went back to Lilly's. Tommy no longer worked there, but a very nice non-Australian-speaking man, who obviously was an expert because his body was covered in ink and piercings, greeted us and listened to our request.

"Sure," he said with confidence. "I know exactly what you want."

An hour later we were back in the parking lot, admiring our new art. On Klutz's right shoulder blade was the Chinese character for "Eternal," and on my left shoulder blade was the symbol for "Love."

At least that's what our skin artist told us. The designs could mean just about anything. We decided it was best that we keep our backs covered if we ever visit China.

Duly prepared for sailoring with our tattoos, we were ready to take on the salty brine.

NINE

Romancing the Waves

We decided that sailing was what we wanted to do. No relying on motors that polluted the air and made a lot of noise. No siree! We wanted to embrace the whole experience of the wind, tall masts, and sails propelling us along large bodies of water.

To do this we vowed that, for once in our lives, we would do it the right way. So we signed up for the three-day-long beginner sailing course offered by the Coast Guard Auxiliary.

It was mid-October 2004, and the last class for the year was being held on the upcoming weekend. Fearing nothing, we geared ourselves up and headed north to a marina on Lake Texoma on the Texas-Oklahoma state line.

An old guy named Captain Gus, who had captained boats for a really long time, was our instructor. He was lean and short in stature with a scruffy look about him—sort of like Popeye the Sailor Man. And he didn't smile much, but that was probably because of all the years he had spent trying to teach landlubbers how to sail a boat. Yet he was likable, in an old codger sort of way.

There were two others in the class. One was Shannon, a thin, dark-haired young woman whose husband signed her up so that they could take their sailboat around the world. At least that's what she said.

Our other classmate, Ted, was taller than Klutz by a few inches and very muscled. He was a nuclear scientist working in Los Alamos, and, yes, it was at the atomic bomb place. He said he chose Texoma because it was easy to get to and had lots of amenities, but I believe he knew what was in the lakes near Los Alamos and made his decision accordingly.

We were an amenable group, at least at first. Shannon probably had the most boating experience due to her weekends of sailing with her husband. Her major concern was learning all the jargon. Klutz, new to sailing, knew the difference between *knots* measuring nautical speed and *knots* as in tying rope. He even knew how to tie a few of the latter.

Ted, who according to himself had a photographic memory, was cool, calm, and collected. Mostly he maintained an aloofness towards the rest of us minions, which after a while even grated on the captain's nerves.

Me? I was clueless and nervous as hell.

The first day was classroom stuff: definitions of boat parts, ropes and knots, and so forth. There was a lot to learn, and most of it made no sense. For example, a boat *shroud* is not something wrapped around a dead person; it is the rigging that secures the masthead. A rope is called a *line*. A *sheet*—not to be confused with the one on your bed—is a special line that attaches to the corners of the sail. An anchor motor is called a *windlass*, and the chain that attaches the anchor to the boat is a *rode*.

Here are more definitions that may prove useful as you continue through the forthcoming stories. *Aft* refers to the stern or rear of the boat. *Stem* is the same as bow or most forward part of a boat. *Port* refers to the left side of a boat, and *starboard* is the right side. But that's only if you are facing toward the bow. Otherwise you and everyone else are confused.

Here is an important one. A *head* is not the thing that sits on your shoulders. It is the toilet.

And maybe the best one: The folks who hang out in sailboats are called *rag-flappers*.

At this point I have to tell you that I have at least one well-documented personality quirk. I tend to ask a lot of questions. Especially the "but why?" kind. Drove my teachers nuts. And Captain Gus was no exception.

By the end of the first day, he was so frustrated with my repeated questions that he was ready to pull out what little hair he had left.

The next morning, at the crack of dawn, we had the written test. I barely passed.

Stupid knots!!!

Klutz did well, but then again he was Army Airborne-trained and had been one badge away from making Eagle Scout. I'm not sure what Shannon scored, but it was better than me. And Ted with his photographic memory scored a perfect 100.

It was now time to put our knowledge into action by practicing various maneuvers on a real sailboat. Afterwards we would each be tested and graded on our execution of these maneuvers.

In near military formation, we trooped down to Captain Gus's sailboat, a thirty-two-foot Catalina, and calmly watched as he guided his jewel out into the open water, reminding us to follow the channel marker's color identification: green on starboard side for going out and red for coming back.

Next each of us took a turn at the helm (aka wheel) and did maneuvers, such as rescuing a man overboard using a weighted basketball named Spalding and giving orders to crew members using correct terminology for all the parts of the boat.

There were a few hiccups, but for the most part things went smoothly.

Probably because we were running on engine, instead of wind.

Bright and early the next morning, we headed back to the marina. As the sun rose above the horizon, the sky turned a brilliant red, which should have been an omen. "Red skies in morning, sailors take warning"—or so the old nautical saying goes.

We paid it no heed. Today was the day we would become sailors—if we passed our last test: captaining the boat under sail.

Klutz and I were excited—and perhaps a little cocky—thinking that this day would be like the previous. We were wrong!!!

This was a whole different experience. The crew nearly fell overboard on Klutz's first jibe, and my man-overboard search-and-rescue turned into a search-and-retrieval because I ran over poor Spalding. Not once but several times! (The poor thing was never the same).

At about noon, the sun disappeared behind a bank of dark thundering clouds, reminding me that we should have heeded the "red sky" warning. Lightning flashed and rain fell in torrents as white-capped waves churned our little boat. Captain Gus barked orders while we scrambled to pull in the sheets, secure the masts, and pray.

Just as quickly as it started, the storm dissipated, and once again blue skies prevailed. Drenched and exhausted, we set the sails, resumed our exercises, and enjoyed the experience of sailing.

By late afternoon it was time for our final test: ready the boat, motor it into its slip at the marina, and dock ... without assistance.

Anticipating completion of the course, we cheerfully set about the tasks of pulling in the sheets and securing the mainsail. When all was ready, we looked at Captain Gus for further orders.

He said nothing. Just stared back. Like the proverbial light bulb, reality dawned: one of us had to man the helm. We looked at each other, our blank expressions revealing our terror.

"You do it!"

"No, you do it. You're better at the helm."

"No, you're better than all of us."

Faced with the dilemma of no volunteer helmsman, Captain Gus decided we would draw straws.

Ted lost.

Showing less bravado than he had the first day, Ted assumed the captain role, assigned crew tasks, and manned the helm. At first it was a little shaky, but Ted managed to maneuver the boat past the breakers and into the marina. Now all he had to do was find the slip and dock.

Shannon's task was port side, handling the dock lines, while Klutz and I were starboard in charge of the *spring lines*. Don't ask me why these are called spring lines when there are no springs, just a coiled rope on the dock.

We were supposed to grab these lines from the dock and wrap them around the *cleats* (not the same as cleats on sporting shoes) as Ted eased the boat into the slip. This was a relatively simple task, and, in an alternate universe, it might have worked.

In our universe, however, it all went to hell in a handbasket. Ted nosed the bow forward, but at an angle and a little too fast. To slow the forward thrust and adjust the stern, he needed to reverse the engine. But instead of reverse, he revved the engine forward.

To be fair to Ted, the spring lines that Klutz and I were supposed to grab would have halted or at least slowed the boat's forward motion. Unfortunately we couldn't find the spring lines.

The ensuing crunch was not a good sound to hear.

All the while, a gaggle of rag-flappers were relaxing in lawn chairs on the pier, sipping some adult beverages and watching the drama unfold. Horror registered on their faces as the bow of the boat careened into the pier near their feet, and they fell over their gear and ice chests as they stampeded to get out of the path of the runaway vessel. I thought I might have to perform CPR on poor Captain Gus.

Later we found out that a prankster moved the spring lines from the starboard to the port side of the dock. But that didn't change anything for Captain Gus. He resigned. He was done trying to teach "idiots" the art of sailing.

Klutz and I, together with Shannon and a very subdued Ted, somehow got passing grades, maybe for not sinking the boat or collapsing the dock. Whatever the reason, we were now certified sailors.

Now all that the Klutzes needed was a boat.

Since we were not quite ready to buy, we signed up for a timeshare-type ownership on a beautiful thirty-six-foot Hunter sailboat docked at that same marina. It would be a good starting point for our maritime adventure because the owner of the boat used a computerized checklist to make sure everything was properly readied upon arriving and leaving. And because there was a long list of must-do items before leaving dock, this checklist was a great help.

We soon discovered that boat timeshares don't work unless the boat is available when you are. All the normal nonworking hours were already booked up.

Then we learned that we couldn't bring our dogs. That became an instant deal breaker.

And so we did what any predictably unpredictable Klutz would do. We bought a sailboat.

TEN

The Birth of Martini Alley

She was a 1998 Beneteau yacht, thirty-six-feet long with a twelve-feet-wide beam. She was built to sail.

The cockpit and helm were aft, and a four-by-five-foot hatch opened down to the lower level by way of a ladder. The below deck held fore and aft berths, a galley with a booth-type dinette, and a head with a sort-of shower. Teakwood decked the interior, and even though she needed quite a bit of cleaning, she was simply beautiful.

And she was ours.

She was registered in Texas as *Family Affair*, but because Klutz and I like martinis—gin martinis—we decidede to call her *Martini Alley*.

The only problem was that our new baby was docked at a marina across Lake Texoma from the one where we had a slip. And because Klutz and I were sailing novices and knew nothing about how our new boat handled, we were reluctant to move her without assistance.

To our relief, the broker who sold us the boat assured us that he would accompany us to her new berth and provide hands-on instructions on how to sail her.

Then he reneged. On the appointed day to take possession of our new pride and joy, we arrived at the marina and were handed a note saying the broker couldn't make it. I was almost in tears as we sat in *Martini Alley*'s salon considering our plan of action.

Not one to ever ponder for long, Klutz jumped up and announced, "We're going to move her ourselves. I know we have no clue about how to work this boat. I know we must traverse the Red River and get around all the sand bars, tree stumps, and other topographical nightmares."

I started to say something, but Klutz held up his hand signaling me to be quiet.

"As I was going to say," he said with a dramatic sweep of his arm, "we are officially certified by the Coast Guard Auxiliary as **sailors**. So what could possibly happen that we're not prepared for?"

Apparently, a lot ...

Just maneuvering *Martini Alley* out of the slip was difficult enough, but figuring how to work the lines was next to impossible. The sheets wouldn't cooperate at all because one of the winches was slightly bent. Within thirty minutes, Klutz and I were screaming at each other like salty sailors.

We could have simply motored across the lake. But because we are, first and foremost, Klutzes and because this was a *sail* boat, not a *motor* boat, that option was never even considered. We *had* to sail it.

So sail it we did.

Six hours later—for a trip that should have taken only two—we approached our marina. Neighboring boat owners stood on the piers waving and cheering. *Martini Alley* was almost home.

Those celebratory cheers quickly turned to gasps of utter horror as the gathered rag-flappers watched us weave wildly past the channel markers and head into the marina. *Martini Alley* careened past their slips, barely missing the bows and sterns of the docked boats. Twenty or so people tripped over each other trying to protect their vessels from the mayhem.

It would have been great slapstick humor in a Charlie Chaplin movie. But it wasn't. It was real life, and we were the unwilling stars of the show.

Calmer heads than ours came to the rescue, and without too much damage *Martini Alley* was maneuvered into her berth. No insurance companies needed to be called.

I learned many things on that first trip. For example, I didn't know a sailboat could do consecutive 360-degree pirouettes. It can.

Another interesting insight: if you look out the galley porthole and see only the feet of a heron submerged in the water, you are about to get stuck.

But mostly I learned that sailing folks are forgiving—because they've been there themselves.

They don't judge.

They just drink!

A lot!

Despite our inauspicious beginning, we enjoyed *Martini Alley*, especially when we didn't move it out of the slip. Being lulled to sleep with the gentle rocking of the boat, hearing the shrouds slap against the mast, swimming off the stern. and, of course, enjoying the never-ending cocktails with fellow flappers was everything we had hoped for.

It was taking her out into the lake that caused problems. For instance, sand bars were notorious for shifting locations in the Red River, but they couldn't hide from us.

No matter where they moved, we found them. I think the tow company owner made so much money from pulling us off sand that he was able to retire after the summer.

And then there was the time Klutz tried to steer our twelve-foot-wide boat into a twelve-foot-wide slip meant for dinghies or jet skis. The sound emitted by *Martini Alley* was a cry of agony as her entire starboard side scraped against the cement bulkhead. That was costly.

Add equipment, maintenance, marina fees, etc., etc., *ad nauseam*, and we can attest to the saying that BOAT really is the acronym for "Break Out Another Thousand"—or, in our case, "ten thousand."

Our sailing adventure came to an end the next summer when we moved from north Texas to Corpus Christi's North Padre Island. Klutz wanted to have *Martini Alley* hauled down to the coast, but I wasn't sure I was ready to tackle her, Klutz, and the Gulf of Mexico all together and at the same time.

So we sold her ...

ELEVEN

The-Boat-With-No-Name

...and immediately bought another boat.

Not a big one. Just a twenty-foot outboard motorboat. And we didn't name this boat *Martini Alley II*. In fact, we didn't give it a name at all. It didn't seem big enough to have a name.

Despite my memories of our Lake Texoma misadventures, I was excited to get back into the water—or at least into the canals. Should we venture there, Laguna Madre was wide enough to prevent us from ramming into another boat, and the top speed to canal crawl was 5 mph. How could we possibly get into too much trouble? We were ready with bait, tackle, and a cooler filled with adult beverages.

Before we could do all this fun stuff, however, we had to maneuver the trailer holding our little *boat-with-no-name* into the water. The job required a calm, experienced "pilot" at the wheel of the towing vehicle and a "wingman" behind the boat trailer to signal directions. Since the idea of standing behind the trailer as it backed into the water scared the heck out of me, I got to be the pilot.

The boat trailer was hooked to Klutz's Jeep Wrangler, which, as any true Jeepster knows, has a manual shift—a very-hard-to-shift manual shift. And the clutch was so far forward that just reaching it with my squatty legs was almost impossible.

I had to sit on the very edge of the driver's seat and then, while leaning back, stretch my left leg far enough forward to push in the clutch. In this position, however, I couldn't see over the steering wheel. I felt like I was trapped in some medieval torture contraption.

I thought I knew how to drive a manual transmission vehicle, but the Jeep proved me wrong. It seemed to me that the gear shift positions were in the wrong place, which made the Jeep go forward when I wanted it to go backward or backward when I wanted it to go forward. Or I would just sit there, yelling obscenities, while grinding the gears and going nowhere at all.

As difficult as wrangling that Wrangler was, there was also the matter of the twenty-foot-long boat trailer. It had an evil mind of its own, and it was out to get me.

There stood Klutz in the water, directing me.

"Turn right," he yelled.

I did, but the trailer went left.

"No," he hollered, motioning with wind-milling arms, "Turn right!"

I screamed out the window, "I did turn right. The stupid trailer didn't listen!"

And so it went. I turned right, and the trailer turned left. Or if I turned left, the trailer went right. It always went in the opposite direction than where it was supposed to go.

One time the trailer turned so far right that I could see the back of the boat through the passenger window. It was a perfect jackknife—a flawless **10** on the Olympic judges' scorecards!

Simple directions turned to screams and shouts, accompanied by more arm-waving than a New York City traffic cop. If Klutz thought his flailing arms meant something like a signal about the trailer, he was grossly mistaken.

Thankfully for our marriage, a kind soul eventually came by to help, and in due course *the-boat-with-no-name* was bobbing in the water. The ensuing hours were spent merrily motoring around the canals and small stretches in the Laguna Madre while trying to forget the launching debacle.

Inevitably we had to leave, which required doing the reverse of getting into the water—the dreaded backing of the trailer, accompanied by more arm-waving and yelling. For a boat with no name, a lot of names were thrown around—most of them rated for mature audiences only.

My takeaway: truck drivers go to driving school to learn how to back big trailers.

Sign me up.

Regardless of the difficulties, we did have some good times tooling around in *the-boat-with-no-name* ... when the motor worked. And except for the trailer thing, it was much easier to handle than the sailboat. If we ran aground, it was easy to simply get out and push it back into water.

The most never-to-be-forgotten occasion on *the-boat-with-no-name* was when our friends Cindy and Jim came to visit. It was December 31, and we decided to pack a cooler with drinks and munchies and head to the water for a run-up to New Year's Eve. The boat had just been released from the shop after repair of an engine issue, so we considered ourselves good to go.

Having owned a small motorboat with a trailer years ago, Jim performed the trailer-maneuvering thing without a bit of yelling and flailing arms. Our little boat was soon in the water. We climbed aboard ...

... and that was as far as we got.

The motor wouldn't start.

The-boat-with-no-name was going nowhere. Not only was it going nowhere, but it was also blocking the boat ramp so that no one else was going anywhere either. While we were alternately cussing and cajoling the sputtering engine of ineptitude, twenty or more vehicles with boats in tow were soon lined up on the ramp—waiting ... These eager, but not-so-happy, boaters soon joined in the effort to get our motor started, without success.

Since we didn't bring oars, removing the boat from the water was the only option. So with grunts and groans and coarse language and a multitude of suggestions (including the fastest way to sink the damn thing), the trailer was once again backed into the water, and the boat was pulled by hand onto the trailer and hauled away from the ramp.

Hoorahs filled the air as the remaining boaters queued up for the ramp once more.

It was what happened next that made this boating story so memorable. After Jim and Klutz moved the Jeep, trailer, and attached boat away from the ramp and into a safe parking space next to the canal wall, the four of us climbed aboard. And then, just for fun, Klutz dropped the anchor over the side where it landed with a thunk on the pavement.

Soon Jimmy Buffett music filled the air as we commenced to break out our snacks and toddies. As we sang about lost shakers of salt, proposed many toasts to the soon-to-be New Year, and waved at folks on and off the water, our boat party soon brought out a crowd of kindred revelers who added their own toddies and song to the mix.

Returning home later, we all agreed ...

This was the best boat trip ever!

TWELVE

The Return of Martini Alley

Not long after our land-locked on-board New Year's Eve revelry, we sold *the-boat-with-no-name*. However, that didn't mean we were done with boating.

Oh no!

The open water continued singing her bewitching siren song, and like Odysseus and his seafaring crew, we couldn't resist the call.

For Klutz it was the beginning of a new mission. He set out to find **The Perfect Boat**: one that would allow us and our dogs to travel via the Gulf of Mexico to the Virgin Islands or up the Mississippi or even cruise as far north as the Great Lakes.

Klutz tackled his boat quest like Ahab took on Moby Dick. The Texas, Louisiana, Alabama, and both Florida coasts were explored and re-explored to no avail. Never a quitter, he threw caution and money to the wind as he searched, knowing eventually he would prevail.

Then, on one fateful day, he found it. She was a trawler built by Trojan Yacht Manufacturers: forty-two-feet long by fourteen-feet wide. She had four levels: a stand-up engine room in the hull, galley/living area with forward and aft cabins, a main deck, and finally a flybridge.

She was a beauty ... or would be after her makeover. It would take work and a boatload of money (pun intended) to make her shipshape for travel and living aboard. But we were undeterred. Obviously we had long forgotten the "This Old House" remodeling experience.

Damming all those torpedoes, we plunged full speed ahead, bought her, and officially changed her name to *Martini Alley*.

After months of cleaning, replacing flooring with teak, repairing the four diesel engines, rewiring the electrical system, replacing the GPS and radio system, installing new Bimini tops, adding enclosures on the sun deck and flybridge, and so much more, our lady was ready to leave the shipyard near Galveston.

Our course and destination? Southwest via the Intracoastal Waterway to her new home at the Padre Island Yacht Club.

Now all she needed was a full tank of fuel.

Okay, this is probably a stupid question, but do you know how much it costs to fill a six-hundred-gallon fuel tank with diesel? Or how many gallons a trawler that size could consume on a cruise?

We sure as heck didn't. Let me just say that a two-hundred-mile cruise with **four** diesel engines averaging **1/2 mile per gallon** at a cost near **$4.00 per gallon** was, ah, a bit more than we planned.

Did I mention the **six-hundred-gallon** fuel tank?

I'll let you do the math because I get light-headed around all those zeros.

It was finally departure day, and Klutz and I, along with our canine crew, were ready. Winfred and Jack, two boat captains who had been working on *Martini Alley*'s repairs, accompanied us. Loaded with tons of food and even more libations, we started the engines, checked all circuits and controls, made sure all pumps were functioning, and pulled up anchor.

Our lady, however, had other ideas, because once we were underway, things that had been working suddenly stopped—and then just as suddenly restarted. It wasn't everything at once, just now and then, but it was enough to be aggravating.

Captains Jack and Winfred couldn't figure out what was wrong. They shrugged and simply chalked up her fickleness to the boat's female gender, but their logic was less than convincing. Whose bright idea was it to label boats as female anyway? In my opinion, *Martini Alley* was acting like a spoiled brat. A male spoiled brat.

Nonetheless cruising down the waterway was an idyllic adventure. Dolphins swam circles around us while seagulls hovered over the stern, swooping down to snatch fish churned to the surface by the *screws*, better known as propellers. Wildlife, skittering along the barren land on both sides of the Intracoastal Waterway, added to our entertainment.

Several days later and with great fanfare, *Martini Alley* and her crew arrived safely at her new home. It was a tight fit, but with lots of help and advice from onlookers, she was reversed into the slip without mishap.

Knowing that true boaters are a superstitious lot, Klutz and I decided to take no chances with this vessel. We held an "Official Christening Celebration" the very next week.

Drinks flowed while guests toured her beautiful decks. Everyone agreed that she was one beautiful lady. As we raised our champagne glasses for a toast, Father Doug, our friend as well as our priest, bestowed the blessing. We registered her, and so, in the eyes of one and all and the state of Texas, she was christened *Martini Alley*.

Sadly, that was the big boat's finest moment.

THIRTEEN

Martini Alley: *The Final Voyage*

Before recounting this cautionary tale of high-seas daring, I would like to offer this preamble:

You will not be able to rent this epic of Coast Guard heroics on Netflix.

No animals were mistreated or harmed, and the human injuries proved to be relatively minor, except to our egos.

The emotional toll, however, was another matter. In the end, a seafaring romance would crash on the rocky shoals of irreconcilable differences.

Now to the story ...

Klutz and I were cruising our girl from Port Aransas, Texas, to Kemah, Texas, for needed repair work.

More needed repair work!

Captain Jack, who had continued working on the boat, and his wife Sally Ann also were going.

Small problem. Sally Ann didn't like being on a boat, except when docked, and she really didn't like open water.

We assured, reassured, and re-reassured her that, according to the maritime weather station, the winds were going to remain calm throughout our trip. In addition, we told her that we were going to cruise only in the Intracoastal Waterway and that the journey should only take twenty hours.

All would be well, we promised.

The first clue that all might not be well occurred the day before our planned departure—the forward marine head stopped flushing. But we still had the aft head, so no major problem. With prudent use, all would still be well.

The second clue was supplied the next day as we were getting ready to pull anchor to leave the marina. When Klutz opened the electric box cover to extract our power cords, he saw that the connector to the main cord was seriously burned. That's probably why our electrical circuits kept shorting out.

Captain Jack fixed that, and even though it was now early afternoon, and we were minus one head, we decided to take off anyway. We unhooked from the dock, and soon we were in the channel and gleefully anticipating a wonderful trip.

Cruising progressed calm and smooth for, oh, something like, ah ... thirty minutes. Then the newly rebuilt port engine started sputtering.

Then the wind picked up, making the water choppy, and Sally Ann's eyes began to grow wide as she surveyed the less than all-is-well conditions popping up around her.

It was nearing five o'clock as we approached Port O'Connor, and we had not made much headway on reaching our goal for the day. But this was the last marina before entering Matagorda Bay, and there were less than two hours of daylight left.

Decision time. Should we stay, or should we press on?

All three of us looked at Captain Jack. After all, he was the expert in this field.

"There are plenty of inlets along the Intracoastal that are deep enough for us to pull into and drop anchor," he said resolutely. "I vote to go on."

Literally throwing caution to the wind, we agreed to keep cruising onward. After all, we had a new generator, a working air conditioner, good batteries, lights, one functioning head, and so on and so forth.

Remember the line "Stupid is as stupid does" from *Forest Gump*? This phrase popped into my mind as we resolutely motored forth.

As luck, or lack thereof, would have it, dusk was rapidly approaching, and we had not found a cove deep enough for us to enter. Again and again, we ran onto sand even if we moved a few feet out of the center of the channel. Back at Port O'Connor we failed to consider the effects of tides within waterways next to the Gulf of Mexico, and now we were smack dab in the middle of low tide.

Sally Ann was seriously not happy. She kept running her fingers through her short brown hair and muttering about how her life was ending.

I was navigating and Klutz was at the helm when we both noted a green buoy marker at the edge of the channel. We eased past it on our starboard side but didn't get far until we hit sand ... again.

Tired and cranky, I called to Captain Jack to see if he would power us off the sand. He was obviously cranky too, because with a loud growl he grabbed the helm from Klutz. Clutching the wheel in one hand and the controls in the other, he threw the engines into a full-throttle reverse. As we all stared, unable to move, mouths agape in shock and horror, *Martini Alley* careened backwards straight toward a looming channel marker.

Jack tried to correct the direction, but it was too late. A deafening sound erupted underneath our feet as *Martini Alley* lurched to a grinding stop.

Sally Ann leaped to the deck railing. I thought she was going to throw herself overboard, but instead she shrieked, "What the hell just happened?"

The rest of us wondered the same thing as we stared at the green buoy bouncing against the stern. With cold sweat running down my back, I watched as Klutz sprang into action. My brave ex-combat veteran war hero jumped into the water—and landed, feet-first, in bottom muck.

Positioning himself first on his knees, he proceeded to lay flat on the slimy bottom and then ducked his head into the murky water to scope out the propeller and as much of the hull as possible.

After what seemed like eternity, he climbed back aboard covered head to toe in black muddy goo. His report was equally dark. By the look of things, the speed of the reverse caused the buoy chain to wrap itself several times around the starboard propeller shaft and pull us onto another sandbar even closer to the main channel than our first grounding.

The fact that the low tide was beginning to reverse didn't make a difference. *Martini Alley* was not going anywhere. We really were dead in the water.

The moon and stars hid as darkness enshrouded us. The propeller wash from passing barges added to our misery as our vessel slammed against the buoy.

Then the wind increased. The boat rocked so much that walking around was like riding one of those mechanical bucking bulls.

Then the generator stopped.

And finally, as if on cue, the one working head ceased to function.

This was not ending well.

While Klutz inspected the exterior and interior of the hull, I radioed the Coast Guard to alert passing barges that we were close to the channel and stuck. Heaven forbid we get clobbered by a wayward barge.

We had life left in the boat's batteries—but not much—and that meant our cell phones, along with all of the boat's electrical systems, would soon be out of power. Jack had the most battery storage left in his cell, so he was put in charge of coordinating with the boat towing service.

"Good news," he said. "A tow boat is on its way." Without skipping a beat, he added, "Bad news. It will take a minimum of three hours to reach us."

Sally Ann, whose emotional status had been deteriorating steadily, was now in full panic mode. She was hyperventilating and dry-heaving, even after taking the maximum dosage of Dramamine and ginger.

Cinching her life jacket even tighter did little to help. Every time I radioed a passing vehicle or the Coast Guard, she screamed into the microphone, "**HELP! There's a sick woman on board!**"

Where's the valium when I need it?!?

We eventually convinced Sally Ann to lie down, and she did. But not on the fly bridge or the deck where there was a smidgen of a breeze. Instead she went below deck to the tiny forward V-shaped berth where the air was still, hot, and steamy. Fully enclosed within two lifejackets and clutching all her earthly possessions, Sally Ann was soon drenched with sweat. She looked more like a spinach or seaweed taco than a human being.

But she was still able to scream expletives with supernatural lung power.

By this time, all of us were wearing life jackets, including the dogs. Not that there was a chance of sinking—we were only in four feet of water. But better safe than sorry, as my mother always said.

I took control of the radio while Klutz worked on the generator and Captain Jack attended to Sally Ann below deck. Suddenly an earsplitting clanging noise, reminiscent of bells in an old firehouse, erupted from the bowels of the boat.

"Taking on water," Jack yelled as he opened the hatch to a find a foot of water in the bilge. We had three brand new bilge pumps when we started, but now none worked.

"But we're on top of sand," I reiterated to the Coast Guard operator after explaining our current situation. "So no problem. Right?"

"Negative," the operator responded. "There could be a problem. If the water in the bilge gets any deeper, the boat will lose all battery power."

With a drawn-out breath, he continued. "You see, if there is a breach in the hull, and we pull you off the sand bar into deeper water, the boat would naturally take on water ... and could possibly sink."

My throat constricted—I couldn't breathe.

This was it! We were going to drown ...

... in four feet of water!!!

"Okay," I said to myself in my most persuasive talk-to-myself voice. "If this is the worst that's going to happen, then we will be fine."

At that point all radio communication ceased, except for the one emergency channel. Battery power was next to nothing on two of our four cell phones.

It was nearing midnight when Captain Jack got one of the bilge pumps working. But it was still a "no go" for the toilets, air conditioner, and non-emergency radio channels. Adding to our misery, *Martini Alley* continued to be buffeted by the wake of passing barges.

Mercifully the Coast Guard arrived. While the medic examined Sally Ann, another crew member evaluated our boat and had some positive news. The bilge water was down to six inches, and with the help of an oxygen mask, Sally Ann's pulse and breathing slowed.

The Coast Guard crew remained with us for about an hour, monitoring the ETA of the tow boat and the water in the bilge and making sure Klutz and I would be okay after they took Jack and Sally Ann back to their base at Port O'Connor. They also charged our cell phones.

There was, however, one itty-bitty new question. Where could Jack and Sally Ann stay after they reached shore? They couldn't stay at the Coast Guard office, and because of a fishing tournament in Port Lavaca, there were no hotel or motel rooms available in the area.

"Don't you have any friends you can call to come get them?" one of the crew members asked.

"Not at one in the morning," I retorted.

A quick glance at Sally Ann's ghastly demeanor persuaded me to re-evaluate. When I considered the alternative—Sally Ann staying on board—one a.m. no longer seemed all that late.

Still feeling some reluctance, I called and woke Forest, one of our few friends under the age of sixty-five, and begged him for help. Without hesitation he said okay. Unfortunately, it took him nearly three hours to reach the Coast Guard station where Jack and Sally

Ann waited. Of course, it was another three hours back to his house.

The Coast Guard left us with instructions to check the engine room for water every fifteen minutes. As added reassurance, one of the crewmen called, as promised, every twenty minutes to make sure we were okay.

Meantime, we (me, Klutz, and our two dogs) waited. It was close to two in the morning when the tow boat team arrived. After another hour, *Martini Alley* was freed from the sandy bottom.

We made it to deeper water without problems and dropped anchor. The diver was able to free the buoy from its end of the chain, but the chain itself was wrapped too tightly around the propeller shaft to be removed.

The diver was still working under our boat when the tow captain noticed dark fins swimming close to both boats. As we were in the Intracoastal Waterway, the fins probably belonged to dolphins, but the way our luck was going …

Let's just say that safer seemed a whole lot better than sorry.

Yanking on the air hose alerted the diver, and he scrambled out of the water. He avoided the fins, but just as he pulled himself onto the swim platform, he collided with a huge Portuguese man o' war. The result of this encounter was a painful sting on his leg.

Klutz offered to pee on the sting site, but, for some reason, the diver declined.

When we thought things couldn't get worse, seasickness in all of its copious effervescence gobsmacked Klutz in the pit of his stomach, and soon he was retching up his guts over the railing.

Meanwhile we had to get the anchor out of the water, but the bow switch for the windlass wouldn't work. I ran up to the flybridge and hit the electrical switch for the brand-new, recently installed windlass motor. Nothing. I tried the switch again. This time there were a few sputters before it died.

Along with the boat, the anchor was also dead in the water.

Not finding the breaker or a hand crank, Klutz started pulling the anchor chain (or rode, as it is officially called) out of the water by hand—two heaves at a time. One heave was on the anchor chain. The other was vomit splashing on the deck.

After much back-breaking—and gut-spilling—effort, he finally hauled the anchor into sight. However, Neptune, or whichever sea god was on duty that night, wasn't having it.

The last section of the rode was covered with channel-bottom slime, and, just as the anchor broke water, the rode slithered through Klutz's hands like a snake covered with snot and crashed back into the water.

Expletives, alternating with gastric contents, spewed from Klutz's mouth. Much like the character, Martin Brody, going after the great white shark in *Jaws*, it was now him or the boat.

Gathering all the strength he could muster, he called to the young diver to help pull up the anchor. Five minutes later the anchor, rode, and Klutz lay in a slimy heap on the deck.

Then the long, slow tow to the shipyard commenced. We had been awake more than twenty-eight hours. We were tired, cranky, grimy, sweaty, stinky, and in desperate need of a real toilet.

We arrived at dawn and with shaky sea legs climbed off *Martini Alley*, vowing never to step on its deck again. Just sell the damn thing and never look back—another gripping romance shipwrecked on the sea of love.

I think our dogs agreed.

And so the saga of *Martini Alley* would end.

Or maybe not ...

FOURTEEN

Revenge of Martini Alley

The literary voyage you are about to take is one that never should have been written because there was supposed to be no more *Martini Alley* to write about.

But there was.

And it did ... happen, that is.

But before I begin, I want to reassure you that the Coast Guard was not involved.

However, the EMS was.

When "The Final Voyage" chapter came to its lamentable end, *Martini Alley* was at the boatyard in Rockport, Texas, for major repairs after losing the pulling contest with a channel buoy.

Repairs were mostly finished, and Winfred, the captain who had been working on her repairs, piloted her back to the shipyard in Kemah, near Galveston, for hull work and the other finishing touches awaiting completion.

When everything was as finished as possible, *Martini Alley* was once again moved, this time to a marina to be sold.

Four peaceful months passed without incident—except expenditures of money, and lots of it. Slip fees in the Galveston area were three to four times more than our little boat dock at the Padre Island Yacht Club. On top of that, we had to hire a dock hand to keep her clean—just in case someone was lured into buying her, or at least interested.

No luck, not even a looky-loo. So being money-conscious people with obvious memory issues, we decided our ill-fated trawler needed to come back to Corpus Christi.

I drove Klutz to Kemah and made sure there were provisions for the trip. I was not going because there was no way in hell I was going to travel on that damned boat—ever again.

Since Klutz could not pilot "the boat" (as I now called it because I refused to refer to it by name) the two-hundred-fifty-plus miles back to Corpus by himself, Winfred agreed to come along ... for a "nominal" fee, of course.

Sunday morning at sunrise Klutz, Winfred, and "the boat" left the dock. It was a beautiful day. Nary a breeze stirred the air as mare's tail clouds streaked the clear blue sky. Everything on the boat worked to perfection.

Klutz was so excited with the way she handled and how beautiful she looked that he temporarily took leave of his senses—especially that sense regarding "the boat's" troubled history—and began to fantasize about not selling her at all, or at least selling her only for an absolutely top-of-market price. If nothing else, he would park her and use her as a dock condo or tiki bar.

Of course, all of this so-called "planning" was without my knowledge. (But, in hindsight, the dock condo wasn't such a bad idea.)

All went well, at least so I thought, until Klutz called twenty-four hours later. "Where's the generator manual?" he growled in a not-so-happy voice.

Before I could answer, he yelled, "I found it," and hung up.

Multiple unheeded phone messages later, he finally returned my call. "What's going on?" I asked. "Is everything okay?"

"The newly repaired generator stopped working during the night," he grumbled. "But don't worry. The engines are still purring, so we're going to untie her and take off."

Attempting to hide my misgivings about the outcome of this trip, I pleaded, "Please be careful. No heroics."

"Yeah, no problem," Klutz muttered before he ended the call.

Later that afternoon I noted there was a cryptic voice message from Klutz on my cell phone, "Where's the Dramamine?"

This was not sounding good. I immediately returned his call. Nothing. Not even voicemail. After several failed attempts, I finally got through to Winfred, but I could hardly hear what he was saying.

"What's happening? Where is Klutz?" I shouted.

Winfred shouted back, but all I heard through the howling wind was, "We had ... out into the ... Mexico due to ... the locks on the Intracoastal being ... Fast ... cold ... pushing ... just ... entered ... water. So we ... wrestle our way ... four-foot swells."

"What?" I yelled, now panicking. "I can't understand you. What's going on? What's happened to Klutz?"

" ... spewing insides ... on deck," Winfield responded. "Got to ... "

The connection dropped.

"What the hell is going on?" I yelled at my now silent cell phone.

I called the Rockport Coast Guard and was informed that a set of locks on the Intracoastal was out of commission, and all boats and barges were being detoured into the Gulf of Mexico. At the same time a small craft warning had been issued due to a cold front which was furiously pounding its way into the coastal region, bringing gale-force winds and torrential rain.

"Oh, dear God," I prayed. *"Martini Alley* is out there. Please keep the guys safe."

Meanwhile, *Martini Alley* was lurching wildly with each storm-driven swell. All Winfred could do was grip the helm, pray, and watch Klutz puke non-stop.

Going below deck was not an option, and, besides, Winfred needed help on the bridge. So Klutz curled up on the deck and wished for a swift death. Gone was the happy-go-lucky boat owner of the day before.

The storm swiftly rolled out to sea, and by sunset the intrepid voyagers had traversed through the Matagorda Ship Channel and docked in Port O'Connor. The generator still wasn't functioning, but at least there was no storm damage to the boat. The exhausted voyagers decided the best plan was get some sleep and hope for better fortune next day.

No such luck. Apparently the sea gods were still pissed at Winfred and Klutz because the next morning they discovered the house battery, which was functioning just fine when they docked, was dead as a doornail. To add to their worries, the weather service was forecasting gusty north headwinds.

But the engine batteries were charged and good to go, so off they went.

Not long after they left the marina, the engines started sputtering and intermittently stopping. Combined with strong, unrelenting headwinds, *Martini Alley* was going more backward than forward. One more time the guys had to change their course and destination.

The new goal was Rockport, which under normal circumstances would take three hours or less. However, aboard "the boat," nothing was ever "normal."

Five hours later as they approached the Rockport marina, Klutz called and asked if I would drive over to pick him up. Not a problem. It was only a forty-five-minute drive, and by then they would be docked and ready to leave our Ship of Fools.

I was approximately ten miles out when Winfield called. "How much longer till you get here?!?" He was shouting—again.

Before I could answer to the question, Winfeld added, "He's had an accident."

Obviously he was referring to Klutz.

"What happened?" I asked calmly, thinking he probably crashed the boat into another dock—or boat.

"According to the paramedics," he continued, still yelling, "he needs stitches."

"**What?!?**" Now he had my undivided attention.

In a much calmer voice, Winfred said, "As we were docking, Klutz slipped off the deck and hit his head on the pier, which caused him to fall into the water. He wasn't under that long, and he got out ... eventually."

"My God, Winfred, get to the point! Is he okay?"

"I called 9-1-1 because I couldn't find any bandages," Winfred responded. "He'll be fine. He just needs stitches."

My next question: "Where?"

"Above his left eye."

"Not where he's cut," I yelled back. "Where are you?"

A pause later he yelled, "Rockport marina. **Hurry!**"

When I arrived, I found Klutz below deck. There was a white gauze bandage wrapped around his head, his eye was nearly swollen shut, and his left thigh was minus lots of skin and swollen to nearly twice its normal size.

With Winfield's help, I got him into my car and headed to the nearest minor emergency clinic. On the way Klutz appeared to be okay—until the color in his face turned from white to green.

"I'm gonna throw up," he moaned, leaning his head

out the window. Somehow Klutz managed to hold back until we reached the clinic, and then he up-chucked into a waiting room trash can.

After a quick examination, the physician announced that he could not treat him because the head laceration and vomiting suggested a possible concussion, which required a hospital with trauma facilities. Never mind that Klutz probably swallowed a ton of seawater when he fell off the boat. Or that he had been throwing up for two days due to seasickness.

EMS was called for the second time that day, and Klutz was on his way to the neurology ER thirty miles away in Corpus Christi.

After many tests, X-rays of his leg, a CT scan of his head, and hours spent waiting for the results of said tests, Klutz was pronounced stable. There was no internal head bleeding and no leg fracture, even though by now his leg was swollen to the point I thought it would burst. Thirty external stitches and numerous internal stitches to his head later, we left the emergency room.

On the way home, Klutz looked at me dispiritedly and muttered, "I give up. This boat has it in for me: *Martini Alley*-2, Klutz-0. I don't care what it sells for. We just need to get it **GONE!**"

In retrospect, we should have named this boat *Christine*, as in Stephen King's death-evoking car.

It didn't need a blessing.

It needed an exorcism.

FIFTEEN

Farewell to Martini Alley

A week later, Klutz was still fuming about his near-death experience on *Martini Alley*. Thankfully he recovered without too many ill effects. I mean, he was always a tad crazy, so a little more was hardly noticeable.

True to his word, he turned "the boat" over to a boat broker with hopes of a quick sale.

We were so naive. There was no such thing as a quick boat sale, especially considering the cost of maintaining a vessel this large. This factor alone scared off many would-be buyers.

And then there was her notorious history of breaking down at the worst possible moments, which I had de-scribed in pulse-pounding detail in my two articles, "*Martini Alley*: The Final Voyage" and "Revenge of *Martini Alley*," published in *The Island Moon*, a North Padre Island weekly newspaper.

To my surprise and dismay, the story found its way to Kemah—and the marina where the boat had been moved for sale. Apparently, *Martini Alley* had become a popular topic of coffee shop conversation.

At least the broker was happy because people stopped by ... if only to see if she was real or fiction.

In the meantime, I retired from my teaching position at the university. Since Klutz was already retired, we could go wherever we wanted.

We loved the coast—but on it, not in it—and there were so many places to go and adventures to be enjoyed. The question was: where?

The answer came when our now former son-in-law, an Air Force pilot, was assigned back to the Fort Walton Beach area in the Florida Panhandle. Because of his duties as a squadron commander, coupled with long deployments, he asked if we could come to help our daughter with their kids and the house.

We agreed to go to Florida. It was time for an adventure with the grandkids.

But first we had to sell our house.

And we had to get rid of "the boat," which was still docked at a very expensive marina in Kemah, sucking up more and more of our money. She had to be gone.

Soon!

During one of our frequent conversations about "the boat," Klutz floated the idea of moving her to Pensacola. If we didn't sell our house, he said, we could live on her.

"Hell, no," I responded—other expletives deleted.

After a few days of consideration, I relented.

"This won't be so bad," I told myself repeatedly.

This phrase became my new mantra.

Soon our albatross was on her way to a marina at Santa Rosa Sound, across from Pensacola Beach, but without Klutz or me onboard. Instead we hired a real boat captain to motor her from Kemah to Santa Rosa. He did so ... without a hitch.

Not long after *Martini Alley* arrived at her new home, Tropical Storm Debbie churned her way towards Pensacola and the marina.

"Please God," I prayed. "Please let the storm sink that damn boat to the bottom of the Gulf of Mexico."

No such luck.

SIXTEEN

The Mystery of the Phantom Slasher

Back on land, I was in Florida helping our daughter with her move. Klutz was safe at home in Corpus Christi. Or so I thought ... until he called me a few mornings after the storm passed. He was in the emergency room awaiting the results of another head CT scan.

Klutz tried to sound calm as he recounted his story, or at least as much as he remembered. He said he was with a few of his cronies at a local bar called Scuttlebutts. One beer led to several beers, which led to wine and, of course, more wine. His dinner had been in the liquid form. When he finally decided to go home, instead of accepting a ride or calling a cab, he drove himself.

He remembered getting home without incident and taking his usual nighttime medicines, which included a sleeping pill along with an assortment of other mind-calming drugs. He also said he remembered needing to pee during the night and thought he got up, but he wasn't sure.

"But," I said, interrupting abruptly, "why are you in the emergency room?"

"I'm trying to tell you. There was blood everywhere. **I think I was stabbed!**"

I took a deep breath, and in a composed voice—or what I hoped was a composed voice—I said, "Uh. Okay. Now tell me what happened."

Piecing together the puzzle of what put Klutz in the ER was a mind-numbing experience. There was something about "waking up in the morning surrounded by blood."

"There was blood," he said. "Lots of blood. Blood on the sheets. My head felt like it was splitting into pieces, and I couldn't see out of my right eye."

All that was missing was the severed horse's head.

Continuing his story, Klutz said he needed to get to the bathroom, but first he had to protect himself from whoever or whatever stabbed him. That was the only explanation he could think of for his splitting headache and bloody sheets.

Why someone would break into the house and stab him was the first of many questions in search of answers as Klutz recounted grabbing the sheathed saber that he kept under the bed and stumbling to the potty, shouting to any lurking perp that he was armed and dangerous.

A quick look over his lower body revealed no wounds, but his reflection in the mirror was a different matter. Staring back at him was a strange man covered in blood. There were two, or maybe more, gaping gashes on his forehead, and his right eye was swollen shut.

He was now beginning to deduce—very logically, of course—what had really happened. The intruder hadn't stabbed him. The intruder smacked him in the head with a baseball bat.

That made perfect sense—until he discovered a small pool of dried blood on the corner of the vanity ... and lots more on the floor ... with what looked like footprints or something. He checked his knees and feet and found dried blood smeared there as well.

Klutz then needed to interrupt his "forensic" investigation to do something about his aching, bleeding head. Looking for bandages but finding none, he grabbed a roll of toilet paper and wrapped it turban-style around his head, securing it with duct tape.

Next he checked the doors and windows for signs of entry. All were intact.

I interrupted again, "But what about the intruder? And what happened to your head?"

"Well ... ," he started slowly and then paused. "I, uh, must have passed out on the way to, or maybe from, the bathroom and, uh, hit my head on the corner of the vanity. But I'm not sure."

After managing the toilet-paper bandage, he said he then fed the dogs, found his car keys, and drove across the JFK Causeway to the nearest hospital.

I can imagine that Klutz created a haunting spectacle as he stumbled through the door into the ER with his TP turban and blood running down his face. From my earlier experiences as an emergency room nurse, I was certain that staff members were drawn to the scene like flies to rotting meat.

Klutz said that no one wanted to remove his toilet-paper bandage, but several wanted to take pictures. One of the nurses thankfully intervened.

The CT was as normal as possible, but he did have another mild concussion. When the physician stopped laughing, he warned Klutz to take better care of his head. Several hours and thirty-plus scalp staples later (without an anesthetic), he was released on his own recognizance.

He sent me a picture. His bald head looked like a baseball with two vertical rows of staples extending from his forehead upward. Add a knob to each side of his neck and with all his bruising and swelling, he could fill in as Frankenstein's monster.

While all of this was going on, our boat broker called to say he had a buyer for "the boat." The good part was that his offer was close to our asking price. The bad part was that he wanted to see it first, in Kemah, not in Florida where she was docked.

With a hired captain once again at the helm, we bid a not-so-fond adieu to *Martini Alley*.

And that was it—the end! No more boats!

But wait. Not so fast. You just think that's the end of our boat escapades. There's more ...

SEVENTEEN

No Good Deed Goes Unpunished

Her name was *Bodacious*. She was a thirty-five-foot work boat docked on Bayou Teche, Louisiana, and she was for sale. Although we were still trying to sell *Martini Alley* and another boat seemed like two too many, a good sob story/sales pitch was hard to resist.

And that's where Captain Jack, the guy who helped repair *Martini Alley* and then ran her aground on a sandbar with the prop wrapped up in buoy chain—that Captain Jack!—reappeared. He just happened to be the father-in-law of *Bodacious*'s owner, Billy.

According to Jack, *Bodacious* was used to carry supplies, electrical cable, barrels of fuel, and often crew members out to the oil rigs in the Gulf of Mexico. She had twin two-hundred-fifty-horsepower engines, a center pilot cab, and three two-hundred-gallon tanks: one for water, one for fuel, and one for waste.

"This boat's a real moneymaker," Jack said. "Believe me, Billy sure wouldn't be selling it unless he had to."

Sounding like a TV infomercial ad, Jack continued, "Billy's bad luck is y'all's good luck. All y'all gotta do is buy

the boat and then sell it back to him on monthly installments. Collecting interest, of course. It's a no-brainer."

Even Klutz looked skeptical. "I'm not sure we want to own another boat, even for a short time."

Jack renewed his sales spiel with a vengeance, arms and hands flapping around as if he were getting ready to fly like a pelican on the bayou. "Think of it this way. Y'all will only own it for a day—or at least until the bank clears your check—and then Billy buys it right back."

"Y'all get monthly interest plus a percentage of the revenue he collects from the companies who lease it."

"And when another hurricane like Katrina hits, this boat will be in great demand."

Taking a minute to breath, Jack finished his spiel with a profound, "Y'all be rolling in dough."

I swear, Jack should have been a baseball player because the pitch he threw put Nolan Ryan to shame. And we fell for it, signed the papers for purchase, wrote a check, and, twenty-four hours later, signed more papers for Billy to buy *Bodacious* back—at a low interest rate, of course. At this point, the only one rolling in dough was the attorney.

And, yes, we're suckers—serial suckers who should have a scarlet S tattooed on our foreheads for either sucker or stupid or both—because soon after these transactions, Jack skipped town. Flew the coop. Vamoosed. Not only did he disappear, but he also absconded with our tools from *Martini Alley*.

After three months of payments, Billy skedaddled too—only he took *Bodacious* with him.

We filed charges with the local constabulary, hired a private investigator, and searched the bayou.

Nothing. Apparently both men just disappeared without a trace. Not even the local sheriff could find them ... though, honestly, I don't believe he tried very hard, given that we were out-of-staters—and Texans, to boot.

And so, after ten years of filing charges, obtaining court judgments, and spending thousands on attorney fees and various other legal payments, Klutz and I threw in the towel and called it quits. We did not get back one red cent.

On the bright side, we still own a boat. Don't know where it is—or even if it's still afloat—but somewhere on the Mississippi lurks Captains Jack and Billy, like alligators just beneath the surface waiting for their next prey.

Their bait? Our *Bodacious*.

If the adage about a sucker being born every minute is true, by now *Bodacious* could have hundreds of "owners."

MARTINI ALLEY

and other swashbuckling adventures of a certified Klutz

PART FOUR

Happy Hour With the Sea Gods

EIGHTEEN

Klutz Dives Into the Drink

Jump back from 2012 to the year 2008 and Corpus Christi. Our remodeling debacle by the three amigos was a distant memory, and Klutz was getting restless once again.

Obviously house projects and daily forays to the beach followed by congregating with buddies at the local bar weren't fulfilling enough. He didn't want to launch *the-boat-with-no-name* by himself, and neither fishing nor golfing fit his fancy.

He wanted to do something. If it brought in a little spending money, it would be good. But if it was also fun, it would be perfection.

Even though there were not many fun part-time jobs on the island, Klutz remained undeterred.

Before I continue, allow me to convey a few details about the Padre Island Yacht Club. First, to be a member, you didn't have to own a boat, although ownership gave the member added bragging rights. Or if you owned one in the past, that was almost but not quite equal to current boat ownership.

But everyone's favorite was the member who joined because he/she *wanted* to own a boat. Members in the first and second categories gravitated to these folks like flies to cow doo-doo. Hovering around the unsuspecting newbies, these self-appointed "mentors" sought openings into which to interject their own pearls of wisdom. Or offer a boat for sale.

This feeding frenzy took place during the weekly Friday night happy hour—which usually ended up very happy because all drinks were one dollar.

That's right. Everything from single malt to Carlo Rossi—one dollar. You want a ginger ale? One dollar. Martini? One dollar. Just order and stuff your bill into the jar. You didn't even have to tip because members took turns serving as bartenders. It was a truly wonderful concept. But I digress…

The yacht club sat on tall pylons to avoid flooding water from tropical storms and the occasional hurricane. The top floor housed the main party room, kitchen, full bar, and so forth.

This meant members had to take a rickety elevator or climb one of the two Mount Everest-like flights of stairs to gain access. You always knew when someone with lower extremity arthritis was approaching because popping, creaking, moaning, and groaning sounds preceded their entrance.

Exiting the club had its own set of problems. Courtesy of dollar drinks, most body parts were lubricated enough to dampen noisy joints as well as any pain associated with the stairs. Unfortunately the number of drinks imbibed to reach this altered state often resulted in one or two mishaps. Thankfully no deaths occurred.

It was on one of those Friday nights that Klutz met a retired high school football coach. Coach, as he was called, had a barnacle-scraping business, and it just so happened that he needed help. He wanted to take more time off, but he couldn't because he was the only scraper on the island.

In case you were wondering, a barnacle is a marine crustacean, distantly related to crabs and lobsters, but not mobile. Using the ocean's current for transportation, the parent barnacle searches for hard surfaces (such as whales, turtles, or boats) on which to build their colonies. Once the barnacle finds a nice spot, it excretes a goopy substance from its cement gland and literally super-glues its crusty little body to a surface. And then it multiplies, adding shell upon shell to produce a sharp, nearly impenetrable mass.

Being marine animals, they love salty water. The saltier the better. According to Coach, the water in the Laguna Madre canals contains a higher level of salt than in the open gulf, thus creating a barnacle paradise. Which means that boats docked in these canals accumulate these critters at a rate faster than ants at a picnic.

If left undisturbed, the ever-growing cluster of barnacles would severely damage a boat's prop and hull. Therefore they have to be routinely removed. There were probably several ways to accomplish this task, but Coach said the most effective method was to don diver's gear, go under the boat, and **S-C-R-A-P-E**.

Klutz, however, only heard about half of Coach's job description because he was already picturing himself in fins, mask, and tank—the twenty-first-century version of Lloyd Bridges in *Sea Hunt*.

Without so much as a first thought, let alone a second, Klutz jumped into the barnacle-scraping trade. After all, he was certified as a diver ...

... in 1964 ...

... and in fresh water.

Undeterred by small issues, Captain Nemo, aka Klutz, found his NAUI diver's card, went to the local dive shop to recertify his license, and proceeded to purchase all sorts of diving paraphernalia. Thousands of dollars later, he was ready to go to work.

Klutz quickly discovered that scraping boat hulls underwater was neither as simple nor pleasurable as it first sounded. These little suckers adhered themselves so firmly to the hulls that it required an exhausting amount of physical force to remove them.

In addition, he had to wear a thick-gauged wetsuit and thick metal gloves to protect his skin from the knife-like edges of the barnacles. Within thirty minutes he was not only wet on the outside but soaking on the inside—with sweat.

And then there were the fish that nipped at his legs as they tried to feed on the freshly scraped barnacles. A few of them were so big that he had to physically push them away with a pole.

One afternoon I visited Klutz at work. I could tell what section he was scraping because of the trail of air bubbling on the surface and the swarms of little fish following the bubbles.

It was a truly calming sight, and I was beginning to nod off into my nap zone when a torpedo in the form of a man in full diving gear shot straight up out of the water and grabbed the edge of the pier.

"You won't believe this," Klutz sputtered as he hauled his body onto the dock. "There was this really big fish—I mean **REALLY HUGE** fish—and it grinned at me. Its teeth were like human teeth, and it just swam in front of my face, turned around ... and ... and **GRINNED**."

"Holy shit, I need a beer," he finally gasped as he collapsed in a heap on the dock.

He was right. I didn't believe him. I figured he must have been in the water a little too long and was hallucinating. However, to be fair and give my husband the benefit of the doubt, I researched Gulf Coast fish when we got home.

Believe it or not, Klutz was right. There is a grinning fish. It's called a Sheepshead, has human-like front teeth, and can weigh as much as forty pounds. It is frequently found in the canals because of the abundance of its favorite food: oysters and barnacles. So if someone like Klutz happens to come along and serve up a free meal—and doesn't wait around for a tip—well, what self-respecting fish wouldn't grin?

I made Klutz an extra-large martini and begged his forgiveness for ever doubting him.

Even with all the drama, Klutz loved being in the water. He often reclined on the bottom of our swimming pool with face mask, mouthpiece, and tank strapped on his back. I occasionally joined him, sharing his air tank.

I readily acknowledge that I am not athletic, not a good swimmer—and definitely not into deep-water swimming! The idea of purposely diving fifty to a hundred feet under the surface was more than a little terrifying. In addition, I felt claustrophobic with a mask, mouthpiece, snorkel, wetsuit, regulator, and tank strapped on me.

Nonetheless, it didn't take long before I was "persuaded" to take scuba classes. Despite all my anxieties, I persevered, and shortly after we moved to Florida in 2012, at the ripe young age of 64, I successfully completed my course work and open-water dives. I was an "official" card-carrying diver.

Even though there were dozens of diving groups in the Florida Panhandle, we joined one located near Houston because Klutz knew several of the divers. Soon we were on our way to Cozumel for our first dive trip. Now all I had to do was remember the entire catalog of things required when in the water: check my dive computers and the amount of air in the tanks, descend correctly, ascend correctly, gauge the time spend at each depth, and, last but not least, keep track of my dive buddy.

One very important subject that was NOT discussed at dive school was what to do when you needed to go to the potty while wearing diving apparel. Maybe I missed that tutorial.

Though most dive boats had a head of some sort, tugging off and on a full wetsuit was a pain in the posterior. I heard that most of the guys just peed in their suits—and maybe the gals did also—but that just seemed gross to me.

Then one day, on a particularly cold dive, I felt the urgent need to go—number one. And so I went—pee in my suit, that is—and when I did, my body was instantly bathed in wonderful warmth. Maybe guys weren't as stupid as I gave them credit for.

But doing a number two? I wasn't about to ask.

Over the next year and a half, we took several more dive trips with the group to Cozumel, and for the most part, I enjoyed the experiences. Sometimes the water was clear and warm. Other times it was murky, choppy, and cold, which brought on near-drowning feelings for me and seasickness for Klutz.

It didn't matter though, because being up close and personal to sea turtles, angel fish, and even nurse sharks was more amazing than I ever imagined.

Night dives were especially magical. Stars twinkled above us as we descended into the deep, velvety blue water. Caves sparkled with iridescent plankton, and occasionally an octopus peeked out from behind a rock and then skittered away.

Of course, a chance encounter with a great white or even a barracuda would have been an altogether different matter.

My only real difficulty was descending. I could waddle my way to the diving platform in full gear and jump into the water, or I could sit on the side of the boat and back flip into the water. Not a problem. Once I was in the water, I couldn't descend. I pushed the damned release valve on my buoyancy compensator vest, I blew all the air out of my lungs until I was blue, I wore extra weights, and there I remained, bobbing on the surface like a jellyfish without tentacles.

All the hand and arm movements performed by the other divers—meant to inform me that I needed to descend—only made me more frustrated. Inevitably the dive master would grab my ankle and pull me to the desired depth.

Once I reached a depth of twenty feet or so, I was fine—except for the fogging face mask (not enough spit) and water seeping into my mask. A few times I would start to ascend on my own, without meaning or wanting to, but usually someone would notice me floating away and pull me back down.

I think my buoyancy issues were related to females having more subcutaneous fat, but Klutz said it was because I was full of hot air.

After going on several five-to-six-day dive trips with the group, we were invited to join them on an eleven-day trip to Bonaire, an island located southeast of Aruba and Curaçao, off the coast of Venezuela. The plan was to go in August, because it was off season and the rates were cheaper. Fine with us.

Who would've thought that islands close to the equator have an on and off season? They do, as we discovered not long after arriving. Instead of clear and blue, the water was choppy and murky. The prevailing winds and strong currents made boat diving nearly impossible, so shore dives were the best choice.

However, getting to the water's edge required a fifty-yard hike through cactus and over large boulders while wearing sixty pounds of gear.

To make sure you came out of the water at the same place you entered needed a perfectly working dive GPS and the ability to figure out how it worked. Neither Klutz nor I had a clue. So we stayed close to the more experienced divers.

Did I mention the rocks? There were a lot, and at the end of our dives, I inevitably washed ashore on these rocks—hard-pointy razor-sharp rocks!

On one occasion when a group of us were swimming to shore, I got caught up by the current and became separated from the others. The waves deposited me right on top of the craggy torture devices. Heaving my scraped and bruised body over the jagged outcroppings, I looked and felt like a floundering shipwreck.

What seemed like an eternity later, I spotted Klutz and the rest of our group crawling over the same sharp rocks as waves crashed around them. They appeared more like drunken turtles than divers.

It was a good thing the trip was eleven days because it took at least three to be able to walk normally and another week more for the bruises to subside.

But that didn't stop our diving. No way! We spent thousands of dollars on dive paraphernalia, and, by golly, we were going to use it, even if it meant hanging out in the bottom of our own swimming pool while sipping martinis from a thermos through long rubber hoses.

NINETEEN

Paradise Lost-and-Found

Taking dive trips to the Caribbean was one thing, but Klutz and I began to wonder how much better it would be to live there—and dive whenever we wanted. We had lived in one place for almost two years, and the hankering for new scenery was starting to set in.

Former Corpus Christi neighbors had moved to Belize, and they loved it. But we weren't sure about being that far away.

We were drawn more to the Caribbean and especially to the islands of St. Thomas, St. Croix, and Puerto Rico, because they all were United States protectorates, which meant citizenship wouldn't be a problem. On a cruise several years earlier, we had docked at each of these islands and enjoyed them. St. Croix was our favorite.

St. Croix it would be.

With the choice of island destination made, I searched for a place to stay that was off the beaten path and away from major tourist sites—one that would offer a real taste of island living. An ad on a VRBO website caught my eye.

> ## ROMANTIC ISLAND PARADISE
>
> This affordable air-conditioned bungalow on the beach is perfect for a quiet romantic getaway. Only steps away from the blue waters of the Caribbean, relax in the cooling ocean breezes that surround you in your private island paradise. Fix your meals comfortably in the fully equipped kitchen or taste true Caribbean cuisine in the five-star restaurant located just a short walk down the beach.

The pictures sealed the deal. We put our house on the market, boarded the dogs, and flew to St. Croix. Our mission? To enjoy a romantic vacation on the beach and find our tropical paradise home.

Going from the St. Croix airport to our bungalow was an experience in and of itself. Driving British-style on the wrong side of the road was bad enough, but locating the place was next to impossible. Our off-the-beaten-path destination was exactly that because there was no path unless you call miles of deeply rutted dirt a path. It was a real spine-grinding, head-jarring experience.

Any misgivings we were feeling, though, evaporated upon arriving at our island paradise. The bungalow was one of three attached cottages surrounded by tropical trees, flowering shrubs, and vines in an array of colors.

Inside there was a kitchen, a separate bedroom, and a small bathroom with a shower. As described in the ad, the cottage was close to the ocean, had four walls, a roof, windows, and "cooling ocean breezes." However, the advertisement was less forthcoming about whether those cool breezes actually circulated throughout the house.

The owners, who lived in a separate larger cottage not far from ours, gave us a brief tour of the premises and then left us to enjoy the complimentary basket of fruit and bottle of rum. Cocktails in hand, we inspected our surroundings and concluded that the ad may have been a wee-bit embellished.

For instance, the "air conditioning" described was, in fact, a small window unit in the bedroom, and it worked for only two hours at a time before the breaker short-circuited and shut off. There were two screened windows in the front of the house, but only one in the back, and it was filled with the useless AC unit. So instead of cooling ocean breezes flowing throughout the cottage, we had our own sauna.

The restaurant mentioned in the ad was on the beach and within a short walk from our little love nest. But to walk there, we had to pass a littered, boarded-up five-story condo inhabited by some scary-looking transients.

And the five-star part? Let's just say that four of those stars washed out with the tide.

But the bar was great!

I almost forgot to mention that the bed was not a king or queen or even a full-size double. It was more like a wide twin. We tried sleeping together on it the first night, but with the combination of heat, humidity, and mosquitoes, we quickly decided to take turns each night, one of us on the bed and the other on the sofa. So much for the romantic part of "quiet romantic getaway."

On the matter of mosquitoes, the owner had casually mentioned that a cistern, which supplied collected rainwater for the four surrounding cottages, was located under our bedroom. I imagined a deep dark pool of mosquito larvae breeding under our bed, so I questioned her about the cistern. She assured us that she used bleach regularly to eliminate the pests. Thinking back, my imagination was closer to the truth than she was.

We found the cistern under a throw rug near the bathroom. It was about two feet in diameter and appeared to be sealed by a large wooden lid.

Appearances, however, can be deceiving, as we later discovered while showering in a cloud of steam filled with insatiable blood-thirsty mosquitoes. Neither repellent nor the proffered bug spray thwarted the airborne invaders' mission to attack and destroy. If anything, the chemical deterrents only made those voracious predators more pissed-off and aggressive.

Two nights later, the swarm had become so thick that, in desperation, Klutz and I removed the rug and lifted the cistern lid.

Monsoon season in Southeast Asia was nothing compared to the massive swarm of raptor-sized mosquitoes streaming out of the hole and into the room. It was like standing in a thick fog—only instead of intense moisture, it was a tsunami of densely packed carnivorous insects hell-bent on sucking every drop of blood out of us.

We ran screaming out the door, arms flailing in an unsuccessful attempt to keep the vampire insects from landing on us and draining our bodies.

Hearing our shrieks and suspecting brigands, looters, or worse, the owners came running. By the expression on their faces, I think they were disappointed that the ruckus was caused by plain, ordinary mosquitoes instead of knife-wielding pirates. Nevertheless, they apologized profusely and said they would take care of the problem in the morning.

Klutz and I took sheets and escaped to the beach ...

... where we finally could experience, up close and personal, those touted "cool ocean breezes."

Not only was our romantic getaway a bust, so also was the dream of finding the perfect island home. St. Croix was not the paradise we remembered from earlier excursions. The economy had taken a severe downturn, and the only vibrancy we could find was when a cruise ship docked. Hordes of people flocked into the town for five hours or so and then flocked back to the ship, leaving the island once again deserted. St. Croix as a permanent residence was nixed.

However, we had to do something, because while we were swatting mosquitoes in St. Croix, our realtor called with the news that our house had not one, but three offers. And to sweeten the pot, one of the offers was more than the asking price. The downside was that the buyers wanted to close and move in within three weeks.

Klutz suggested, half-joking, a retirement community in Florida called The Villages. Not joking at all, I jumped on the idea.

"I remember how much fun everyone was having and all the activities," I said excitedly.

"And do you remember all the bars?" asked a suddenly excited Klutz. "Lots of them and just a golf cart ride away. We need to check it out."

Despite the daunting deadlines imposed by the sale, as soon as we got home, we gathered our pets, jumped in the car, and drove eight hours to check out our prospective new utopia.

We loved it. And we could move in immediately.

So back home we went to finish packing.

Movers were scheduled.

Boxes were packed.

Repairs were made.

... and then the unthinkable happened.

Three days before our closing, the contract for our new home fell through—some kind of glitch with the mortgage. In just three short days, we would be homeless, and so, once again, panic descended on the Klutz corps. We sat on a stack of moving boxes, staring into space, contemplating our future living under a bridge.

Suddenly Klutz jumped to his feet and bounded into the kitchen. "I need a drink!" It might have been morning in our world, but in Jimmy Buffett's immortal words, "It's five o'clock somewhere."

I wiped my tear-stained face and yelled, "Pour me one, too."

Taking a couple long gulps of straight-up gin, I asked, "What the hell are we going to do? We have to do something, or we will be on the street."

"No kidding. And just what do you have in mind?" Klutz snapped in response. He was getting cranky.

Silence enveloped us.

After a few minutes, I turned to him and asked, "What about something other than a house? Maybe a trailer or an RV? You know, a land yacht?"

Something in Klutz awakened and, like the Phoenix rising out of the fire, he slowly stood and looked squarely into my face. He was radiant. His eyes sparkled, his face glowed, and a huge smile spread from ear to ear.

"You mean ... " he paused for a moment.

" ... as in we move into and live in a motorhome?!?"

I nodded, and at that moment I knew that another adventure loomed in our future.

and other swashbuckling adventures of a certified Klutz

MARTINI ALLEY

and other swashbuckling adventures of a certified Klutz

PART FIVE
Land Yachting

TWENTY

Hot Wheels

To be truthful, this would not be our first adventure into motor homing. In 1978 we bought a used butterscotch-colored Volkswagen pop-top camper. It was essentially a sixteen-foot van with the capability of unfolding the back passenger seat into a twin bed and "popping up" the van's top to create a second twin bed.

It really didn't qualify as a motorhome because it was only equipped with a two-burner stove and ice box, but no potty. It was perfect for us ... almost.

Because of his height, Klutz was relegated to sharing the upper berth at night with our five-year-old adenoid-afflicted daughter while our thumb-sucking, three-year old daughter was with me on the bottom. Add two dogs, a border collie and a great Dane, and even ear and nose plugs couldn't block the cacophony of sounds and odors emanating from the various creature orifices.

There were a few other inconveniences associated with the van, especially when we took long trips. Lack of space was the major one. But we fortunately discovered that Volkswagen manufactured a tent designed to attach on the passenger-side sliding door, and this was a godsend.

Another issue was the lack of an inside potty. Because our girls were so young, getting them to the outside facilities in the middle of the night or between pit stops was a real nuisance.

I adapted a large bucket with a lid, and it worked perfectly for the girls. I also found it extremely handy for me to use while we were on the road, but Klutz always managed to make a sharp turn just as my bare bottom touched the can's sharp rim.

Despite everything, we enjoyed our Klutzwagen and all the fun we had in it. But after several years, we sold it and switched to a pop-up tent trailer. Still no potty, but we were getting used to the tin can.

Forward from the late 1970s to 2010. We were living in Corpus Christi and, out of the blue, decided that we *needed*—or at least *wanted*—a small motorhome. On reflection, I am not sure why, but at the time it seemed like a good idea.

Klutz investigated the different types and decided that a Class B motorhome would be the best for our needs. Not at all sure what Class B meant, I went with him to a Roadtrek dealership located north of San Antonio. There were many styles and varieties, but the one commonality was the price — **EXPEN$$$IVE**.

A Class B Roadtrek is essentially a van that is outfitted like a camper behind the driver and passenger seats. It has all the amenities needed for camping, only in smaller dimensions.

Arriving midday at the dealership, Klutz and I began browsing the inventory on the lot. We didn't get very far before a salesman suddenly appeared. He was short in stature, a little pudgy, and sported a comb-over hairdo, reminding me of a "before" model for a Men's Hair Club infomercial. Like most salespeople, he smiled a lot, but strangely the smile never made it to his eyes.

After brief introductions he gave us a tour of the various models. Each van was equipped with a small galley that contained a refrigerator, small stove with an oven, and cabinets above a countertop. The toilet had a curtain around it so you could shower and potty at the same time. The back of the van was furnished with a sofa that converted into a double bed, a TV mounted on the wall, and a small closet. An outside roll-down sunshade provided cover and shade over the door.

Klutz and I were impressed, to say the least, but tried to curb our enthusiasm as we trailed the salesman back to the sales building. Presumably to give us the opportunity to talk in private, he retreated into his cubby-hole office.

Klutz turned to me and said softly, "Well, what do you think?"

"These are really cool and would be lots of fun to travel in," I whispered. "But way too pricey. We can't af ... "

A firm tap on my shoulder startled me mid-whisper. "What the hell?" I yelped, whirling around and nearly smashing my nose into the chest of the salesman.

"I know what you're thinking," he said with a huge toothy grin. "Too costly. But we just happen to have used models that I'm sure would fit in your price range."

This guy was beginning to creep me out. First of all, he had to possess the hearing of a bat and, secondly, the stealth of a lion, because neither Klutz nor I heard him approach. Must be a skill taught in RV salesman school.

With a flourish, Mr. Combover turned and pointed to a van that miraculously appeared behind us. It was a Roadtrek 190, meaning it was nineteen feet in length—shorter than the new models that I liked but a little more affordable. And it still had the same features as the new ones.

You guessed right. We bought it and took it home.

The great part about the van was that we didn't have to stop if one of us had to potty, and we could get a cold beverage when desired. It was perfect for road trips.

Very short road trips.

Like to the end of the driveway!

Overnight camping, especially the sleeping part, was not exactly what I expected it to be. Because Klutz needed the outside of the bed to accommodate his height, I was relegated to being cramped against the wall, and I had to crawl over him to get into and out of my sleeping spot. Heaven forbid if I had to pee during the night.

There was also an issue with the generator. A BIG issue. Whenever it ran more than a few hours, the carbon monoxide alarm sounded. This was particularly worrisome when trying to sleep. Even when the alarm wasn't shrieking, the detector's blue light blinked incessantly. We had it checked out several times and were assured that everything was fine.

After the last "no problem" response, Klutz said that I needed to just ignore it because it was now "my problem."

"Fat chance!" I sputtered. "Just you wait and see, we're going to die in this thing."

Aside from the possibility of death by carbon monoxide poisoning, there was an even more odious concern—the black water (aka the poopy/pee) holding tank. To allow enough space for a six-foot person to stand upright inside the van, the designers decided to place the water tanks under the carriage.

The concept itself made sense. Most, if not all, motorhome designs place the tanks there. But the Roadtrek did not have much road clearance to start with. Adding holding tanks with their associated hoses meant that there was next-to-no space between the tanks and the road surface. The likelihood of ripping a hole in one or all of these things on rough or bumpy terrain was almost a certainty.

At the dealership, when Mr. Comb-Over had shown us the undercarriage of the van, Klutz questioned him about the risk of getting a hole in one of these close-to-the-road parts. The man swore on a stack of sales brochures that the chance of this occurring was "almost" zero. Obviously he didn't know the Klutzes.

Disregarding all of these considerations, we outfitted our van for travel and took off for a shakedown trip. Our destination was a state park located a couple of hours west of Corpus Christi. It was a beautiful spot situated on the Llano River. There were huge oak trees, picnic tables, and electric hookups, but no septic or dumping station on site. This was not a concern since we were not planning on a long stay.

After three days, the black water tank was full, and so we readied everything to head home. But first we needed a dumping station.

The closest station was only a mile outside the park. But getting there, we soon discovered, was not easy. The road was packed dirt with gullies so deep that they should have been called ravines.

It was a brain-bouncing experience, worse than the washboard roads I recalled from rural Pennsylvania. Then the road smoothed, and our spirits lifted ...

... *briefly*.

I looked at Klutz and then at the dogs as a foul odor filled the van. It rapidly grew in such intensity that tears pouring like water from an open faucet blurred our vision.

One or both dogs must have had a horrific poop accident. But no. They weren't the source, so I widened the search parameter. Klutz now had his shirt pulled up to cover his nose and mouth and was hollering for me to do something. I didn't have a clue what I was supposed to do.

Figuring the cause had to be outside, I went to the back of the van and looked through the window.

"Crap! Crap! Holy crap!" I yelled as I gazed at a dark brown sludge-like substance trailing on the road behind us. "We are leaking crap! Lots of crap! It's a river of crap!!!"

Screeching to a halt, we both scrambled out and looked under the vehicle. There it was—a gaping hole in the black water hose was emptying the tank.

And I was standing in rapidly pooling feces.

Meanwhile, as Klutz remained on dry ground, I tried to jump to the side, only to slip and fall butt-first in the stinky, slimy shit swamp.

I was in deep doo-doo!

I attempted to stand but slipped down again. Struggling only made matters worse. I just couldn't get out of the yucky muck.

Klutz just stood there laughing so hard that he was nearly doubled over. With all his whooping and hollering, you'd have thought he was watching a Three Stooges comedy fest—and I was triple-cast as Larry, Curly, and Moe.

By now I was on my hands and knees crawling to dry ground while cursing like a drunken sailor.

"I need water—lots of it!" I screamed. "And towels! And clean clothes!"

Never mind that we were on the side of a public road. I stripped off as Klutz, still laughing hysterically, sprayed me with what water was left in our clean water tank.

Wrapped in towels and feeling thoroughly mortified, I got into the back of the van and sat on the floor. Then the dogs started rolling on me. I was done with this whole thing.

The good news was that we didn't need to stop at a dumping station—just a trash can for my clothes. The bad news was that we had to locate a shop to fix the line and tank.

Undeterred after the latest round of repairs, we hit the road again. The sewage problem only raised its fetid head three or four more times. Other than the death by asphyxiation nightmare, it was a lovely vehicle for traveling from one dump station to the next. We just had to work very hard to avoid speed bumps and other such road hazards.

We took the van with us when we moved to Florida in 2012, but we couldn't park it in our driveway, and storage was expensive.

So we dumped it (excuse the pun) at a dealership to be sold to some other unsuspecting mark for the RV salesman's smarmy shtick.

TWENTY-ONE

The Birth of Big Bertha

Now here we were, back in Florida, facing homelessness and contemplating another motorhome—a really big one. Klutz looked at me with cosmic bliss, his eyes spiraling pinwheels of newfound purpose, and I knew without a doubt what was next. I had uttered the magical words—**land yacht**.

Really, though, who hasn't yearned for the open road, traveling from sea to shining sea ... only by land? Being free to wander and explore places of legends only read or heard about—and without the worry of shark bites or drowning.

And the stars!!! Whole constellations of them shining down on us from the heavens as we sit around a campfire every night, roasting hot dogs and sipping martinis, basking in the sweet fragrance of cactus blossoms, and making use of the stress-free serenity to write the next best-seller.

I sighed and said, "What a wonderful experience we could have—crossing America with no worry about finding pet-friendly hotels and places to eat, let alone hauling our stuff into a hotel every night and hauling it back to the car in the morning."

Klutz didn't hear a word of what I just said. He hadn't gotten past the words **"land yacht**." Leaping to his feet, he exclaimed, "Great idea! Let's do it."

By now you probably have figured out that we've never done anything half-assed. Our motto: all-assed or nothing. But for some reason, perhaps due to a flashback to some of our past experiences, I hesitated ...

... for an ever-so-brief moment ...

"Maybe," I said, "we need to take a little more time before doing this. Remember our last motorhome? We didn't keep it very long."

Klutz stared at me incredulously. "Are you referring to the Roadtrek? Number one, that was not a *real* motorhome. And, number two, it was you who had the problem with it. Not me."

I tried to ignore his reference to "number two."

But here we were, only two years after my caca catastrophe, and we once again were talking of buying another porta-potty on wheels—only bigger. Maybe, I thought to reassure myself, this time it would be better.

And maybe the moon really was made of cheese.

My brain was full of questions:
Could we live in something like that full time?
What would we do with our furniture and all our stuff?

I was not ready to sell everything on the possibility that living on the road was going to work.

Klutz was unfazed. To be honest, he was nearly giddy with the thought of buying a large moving house. His eyes sparkled as he searched the web and RV sales locations for the perfect vehicle.

Motorized coach or towed? If towed, trailer type or fifth wheel? If motor driven, gasoline or diesel? Should we plan to tow a car?

So many decisions and so little time.

Following our typically abbreviated selection-making process, we decided on a motorhome type and drove immediately to the closest recreational vehicle store.

A salesman in a golf cart appeared—magically, of course—next to our car. After introductions and our brief description of what we were looking for, he ushered us into his cart and whizzed us through a gate into a football-field-sized parking lot filled with RVs of every size, shape, and description. Overwhelmed by the sheer number of choices, I looked from Klutz to the salesman and back.

"What the heck is all this?" I blurted, finally able to speak. "Did everyone decide to sell at the same time? And is no one buying?"

Blindingly white teeth filled the salesman's face as he turned to answer. "Why, missy," he said in a drawn-out Southern voice that dripped with sweet molasses. "We pride ourselves in keeping the largest inventory of RVs in the Florida/Alabama Panhandle. Anything you want, we got it or can get it." He reminded me of Foghorn Leghorn in the *Looney Tunes* cartoons.

"Well, okey dokey, then," I muttered to myself as we started our tour of wheeled homes. We trekked around the field for what seemed like an eternity and saw nothing that impressed us—or rather, that we could afford—and were ushered into the sales office. The salesman's bright white teeth disappeared, for an instant, and then reappeared bigger than ever.

"This," he drawled, waving a flyer he plucked from a stack on his desk, "is the perfect motorhome for you. It's not yet on the market, but if you buy it now, I can get you a great deal."

With another dazzling display of teeth, he handed us the flyer and cranked up his sermon. "This motor home is top-end, only one owner, low mileage, and it has been garaged. With a price around 90K, it's a heck of a deal."

With the toothsome guile of a shark circling chum, the agent concluded his fifteen-minute-long oration with the come-to-Jesus phrase so famous throughout the world of salesmanship: "This baby won't last long—not at this low low price."

He was right.

It didn't.

Because we bought it.

Our new home was a Newmar Mountain Aire forty-five-foot diesel "pusher," meaning the engine was at the back of the motor home instead of the front.

The fact that it had a hundred-gallon fuel tank and only got about eight miles per gallon didn't faze us a bit.

After all, we had experienced a much bigger fuel guzzler in *Martini Alley*—which held six-hundred gallons of diesel at one-half-mile per gallon.

We were signing the papers when reality slapped me in the face. Leaning over to Klutz, I whispered, "Ummm, we don't know how to drive something this huge."

Klutz was unfazed. "Did you forget" he asked, "that I drove a University of Texas shuttle bus for ten months? And in 1971 I transported elementary kids in a private school van?"

His résumé of driving abilities had grown so much that by the time we signed the papers and forked over almost $100,000 that Klutz was convinced he could steer a Caribbean cruise ship. I wasn't about to remind him of *Martini Alley*.

It was time to leave, but before we made it out the door, the salesman called out, asking us to wait. As we turned, the salesman wrapped his arms around us in a group hug so tight I could hardly breathe. When he let go, I touched my neck, looking for bloody fang marks.

We escaped and almost made it to our car before he caught up with us again. His ear-to-ear grin revealed even more sparkling white teeth than a human mouth should be allowed to have.

"Hey," he said, grabbing Klutz's hand and shaking it like he was pumping up a car jack. "Congratulations. You are now the proud owners of a top-notch motorhome."

Condolences would've been more appropriate.

The next three weeks were spent between the RV park in Navarre, Florida, the service center, and the storage unit. Deciding what to shove into the motorhome and what would be left behind was an exercise in futility. We moved boxes back and forth so often that I swear we transported the same box at least a dozen times.

I approached our departure day with mixed emotions. I would miss living near our daughter, our grandkids, and the beautiful beaches of the Emerald Coast. On the other hand, new adventures were calling, and it was time for us to answer.

First we were going to visit friends near Grapevine, Texas. Next, we were going to spend two weeks in Santa Fe, New Mexico, and finally head to Pagosa Springs, Colorado. After that we would go wherever the road took us.

However, as we were making plans to embark on our travels, we didn't realize that locating a full-amenity RV park with available space big enough for our mother ship was not going to be easy. Most places were already booked, and those with space were far more expensive than I anticipated. This adventure was not going to be cheap.

Be that as it may, deposits were sent, and clothes, cooking utensils, food, dog supplies, essential medical records (human and canine), and everything else we could possibly need were stowed away.

Big Bertha, as we called her, was ready to roll.

Diane's Journal: Day One

We finally began our adventure after a few hiccups, a number of belches, and many—too many—deafening thunderclap farts.

Tess, our neurotic black cocker spaniel, started us off at one o'clock in the morning by distributing a copious quantity of liquid poo throughout the motorhome. She soon followed by vomiting up what seemed like an entire week of doggie food. At three in the morning, Hunter, our other cocker, along with Tess, wanted to go outside. Again!?! Of course, this meant locating their leashes and doggie bags, which I had misplaced after the last outside foray.

A few hours of restless sleep later, we were outside trying to unhook from utilities, attach bikes to Klutz's jeep (which we were towing), and a million other checklist items that had to be done before driving out of the RV park.

Getting the tow bar and jeep hooked together was nearly impossible—probably because we lost the instruction sheet.

Then we couldn't remember where we put the bike attachment. (Getting old is no fun.) Klutz eventually gave up the search and drove to the RV store to buy another one.

By noon we had everything stowed, attached, and secured. We settled into our new home on wheels, happy to be finally leaving.

Tess and Hunter were not happy. As soon as Klutz started the engine, both dogs went berserk and crawled under his feet, prohibiting him from using the gas or brake pedals. I peeled the frightened dogs from the floorboard and tried to calm them as much as possible.

We had not driven far when Klutz abruptly yelled, "Damn it! What's wrong now?" He was staring at the control panel—particularly at the engine light, which was a glowing red beacon. "We gotta get this thing off the road. Now!"

We exited the highway as soon as we safely could, and Klutz checked the now steaming engine. We waited till it cooled enough to drive, then limped our way to the RV shop, which was just a few miles away. By three o'clock in the afternoon, the radiator problem was fixed, and we were off.

Not long after that we crossed into Alabama. That's when Klutz noticed that the horn no longer worked. Neither did the cruise control. And then the passenger seat belt started tightening to the point I couldn't breathe. I quickly unhooked, and the belt retracted into the holder where it became stuck. I had no other choice other than to hold the two quivering dogs in my lap without restraint until we could once again exit.

The horn and cruise control problems were manageable, but the near-epileptic shaking of the dogs was a different matter: it was time for doggie tranquilizers. I briefly considered taking one myself, but instead settled on the sofa with our two drugged dogs and secured the lap belt. Once again we were off.

At about ten o'clock that night it was time to stop. We were frazzled. A truck stop appeared on the horizon, and as we pulled in, the term "boondocking" came to mind. We were now official RVers.

Day one was over, and so was I. No more journaling. I figured that if things continued to progress the way they had so far, I didn't want it documented or remembered.

We eventually made it to Texas without too many more hiccups. After a week's stay near Grapevine and only one trip to the RV repair shop, we broke camp and headed westward-ho.

I had a repertoire of songs waiting to be sung, and as soon as San Angelo was in our rear-view mirror, I belted out Marty Robbins' "El Paso." I desperately wanted to sing "Amarillo by Morning," but we weren't headed that direction. Instead I hummed it very loud, just to annoy Klutz.

Driving through West Texas and New Mexico was more spectacular than I imagined—wide open plains, deserts, and boulders rising from the desert floor. The gigantic red rock outcroppings, miles of cacti, and rivers that begged to be jumped into gave us a sense of awe about the beautiful country in which we live.

Into the second day, I had sung "This Land is Your Land" so many times that Klutz threatened to put a gag in my mouth. But it was the duets with Tess, our cocker, that eventually halted my serenades.

Big Bertha behaved herself: no overheating, no short circuits, no busted lines. Everything was perfect ... until we arrived at the RV site in Santa Fe.

The problem there was not Bertha. It was us and parking. The very notion of reversing this behemoth into a parking spot instilled utter terror in our collective soul.

Couldn't do it. Wouldn't do it. We always made sure our overnight stays involved drive-throughs only, meaning driving forward to park and forward to leave.

But no such luck in Santa Fe. It was a back-in-only site. Klutz and I gazed in disbelief at the narrow strip where our motorhome was supposed to fit. With slow deep breaths and undaunted determination, we unhitched the jeep, and Klutz climbed behind the RV's steering wheel, while I positioned myself in the rear to provide guidance.

As Klutz raced the engine and clunked gears, I waved my arms and shouted directions. I pirouetted and contorted my torso left and right, up and down, trying to give Klutz the right angle. I think I even tried to stand on my head. But we could not guide Bertha into her berth.

No longer talking to each other, we were glumly standing next to Big Bertha when a miracle arrived in the form of the RV park owner. Without a word, or even a smirk, he motioned Klutz to stand aside, positioned himself behind the wheel, and smoothly reversed Bertha into place. Still silent, he exited the vehicle, gave us a slightly amused smile, and walked back to his office.

After a blissful week, it was time to head on to Colorado. Crossing the flatlands towards the mountains was exhilarating, and soon I was singing John Denver songs in anticipation of a Rocky Mountain high. As we ascended into the forest, however, my joyful tunes turned into gasps of fear when I realized how narrow and steep the roads had become.

I couldn't catch my breath and was grasping the dashboard so hard that my knuckles turned white. I prayed for things to get better, but they didn't. The skinny roads with guardrails morphed into trail-like roads with no guardrails. Shoulders narrowed from next-to-nothing to a plunge down the sheer face of the mountain. Instead of looking out of my window at flora and fauna, I stared out into the abyss. Our butt cheeks were sucking up upholstery as Klutz maneuvered Big Bertha around the mountain switchbacks.

And then the truly unthinkable happened. Chugging halfway through a blind curve, we met another RV on the road heading straight toward us. The other driver swerved hard right, probably scraping against the rocky wall, while Klutz inched us even closer to the edge than we already were. Peeking through squeezed-shut eyelids, I watched in horror as pebbles tumbled down the cliff into the bottomless ravine below.

Thinking of the final scene in *Thelma and Louise* I begged, "Please, dear God, let there be something to catch us when we roll off the edge."

We made the turn and breathed a short-lived sigh of relief. Many more switchbacks and more oncoming traffic would confront us as we inched our way up the narrow mountain road to Colorado. My hands were cramped from gripping the dashboard, and by the time we made it to Pagosa Springs, we were stressed to the max limit, no longer talking, and much in need of an adult beverage—or three.

But first we had to find the RV campground, which was located a distance from the town. We eventually found it and checked in.

Fearing a similar parking issue as we had in Santa Fe, we approached our site with trepidation. I wasn't sure if I could take the stress if reverse parking was required. Tears of joy sprung to my eyes because it was a pull-through.

On to that adult beverage.

The RV camp was great, even if it was too remote for cell service. If you really had to make a call, we were told that we could walk up to the main highway, hold the phone very tightly in an outstretched hand, and yell. We were also told to beware of eighteen-wheelers whizzing by so fast that they could suck the phone right out of your grasp.

The inconvenience of cell service paled in comparison to the openness of the woods surrounding our site and by daily visits of deer and other wildlife. Our male cocker spaniel Hunter was really impressed. At least once a day he tore loose of his leash and bounded merrily after a white tail, be it deer or rabbit.

That meant one or both of us had to capture him. Running through chest-high grass was not fun, especially when the result was bruised knees and cut shins from stumbling over rocks and crevices. I swore that I was going to do severe damage to that dog one of these days. That was if we ever found him.

True to form, Klutz and I decided that Pagosa Springs was the closest thing to heaven that we had ever been and soon started scouting condos or land to buy.

Who cares about beaches, sun, and open water when you can have mountains, cold wind, and snow?

Okay, the cold and snow we could do without, but maybe we could do both. Be winter Texans. This could be the start of a whole new adventure.

But first we had to evaluate our current adventure. We had a big motorhome, but can we live in it four to six months out of the year? So far it wasn't working so well, and only two months had elapsed. It was far more stressful than we had expected.

The issue was not just living in close quarters. We also had to attend to Klutz's health and medications, which required us to travel to the Veterans Administration clinic in Albuquerque several times. He had been with the VA system for many years, both in Texas and Florida, but not in New Mexico. Because of that, the Albuquerque clinic could not provide all the help he needed. Evidently there was no universal VA system.

Thinking about finding a condo or lot in one town, even if it was the heavenly Pagosa Springs, defeated the purpose of buying Big Bertha in the first place. We wanted to see our country from sea to shining sea, not just to stay in one or two areas forever.

On the other hand, setting up camp on arrival and then tearing it down when leaving was a proverbial pain in the hiney.

But mostly it was the money. Even if medical matters had not been an issue, the price and availability of diesel fuel, along with the fees for RV parking, dropped a whup-ass of reality on our plans to cruise the country. On top of that, we had the expense of storing our other car and furniture halfway across the country. This cheap-'n'-easy style of living was turning out to be neither cheap nor easy.

Facing reality was hard for us—being dreamers and such—but we had to. The best thing for us would be to go back to Florida, sell the RV, get my car, move into the rental condo that we owned in Corpus Christi, and try to recoup our losses.

We headed our land yacht out of her moorings and set sail along Interstate 10 to Pensacola. Fifteen hundred long miles later we returned full-circle to our original starting place—the RV dealership and our old friend, the toothy apostle of sales.

By the time we got there, the dogs weren't even talking to us, and I certainly wasn't singing—though I must confess that Willie Nelson's "On the Road Again" filtered through my brain rather often.

Against all odds, Big Bertha didn't give us one bit of problem along the three-day trek back—she probably wanted to get rid of us as much as we needed to get rid of her. Nonetheless, we bid her a bittersweet farewell, said hi and goodbye to our daughter and grandkids—again— and headed back to Texas.

We weren't sure what we would do or where we would go, but Texas was as good a starting place as any.

Over seven years have passed, and, aside from moving from South Texas to Central Texas and then to North Texas and back to Central Texas, our life has been pretty boring. We've not bought a single boat, RV, camper, or anything adventurous. We even sold our SCUBA gear.

So the all-embracing question of the day remains ... Are we ready to retire the Klutz roadshow?

HELL NO!!!

and other swashbuckling adventures of a certified Klutz

MARTINI ALLEY

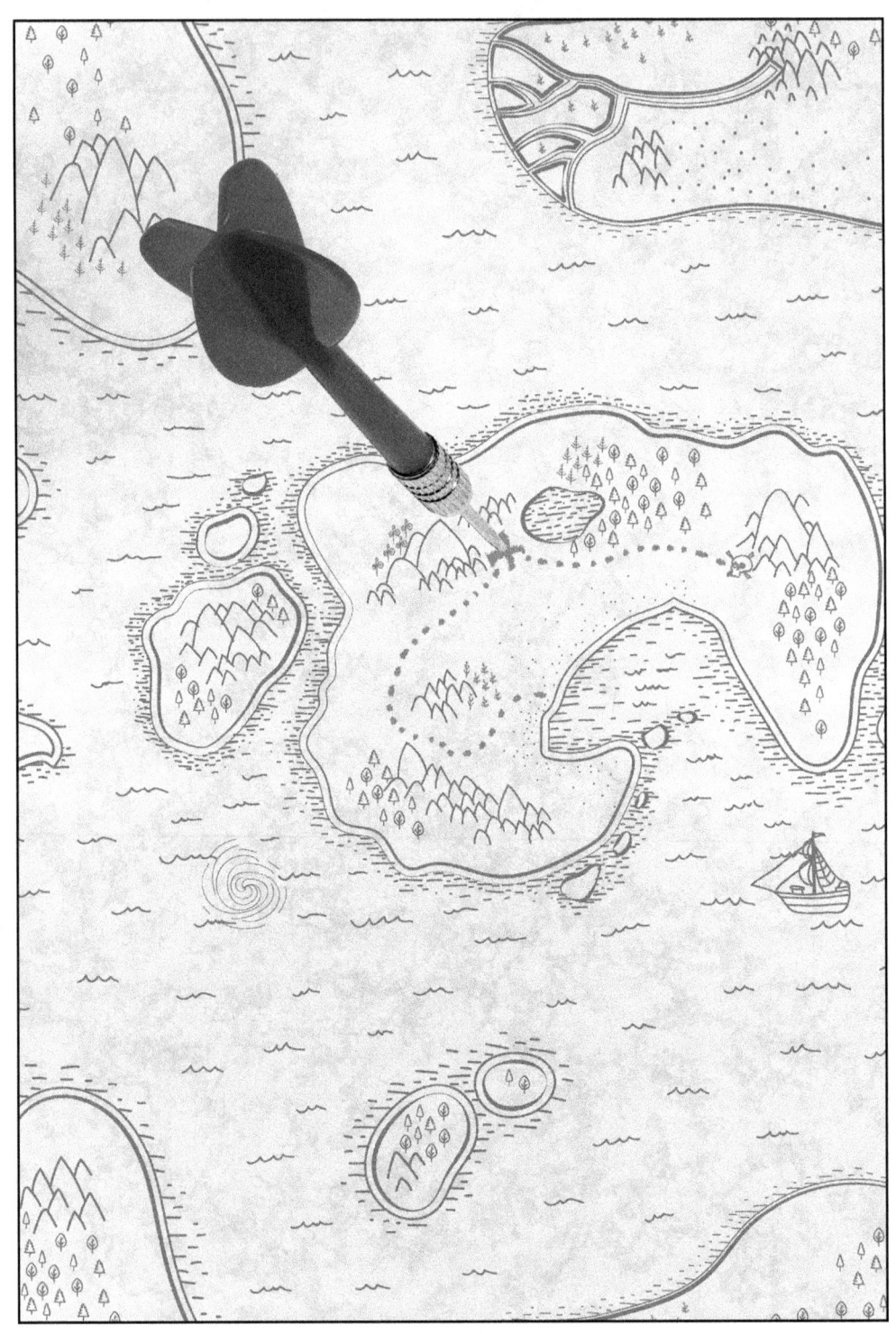

and other swashbuckling adventures of a certified Klutz

PART SIX

Epilogue: Where Next?

TWENTY-TWO

Sailing into the Sunset

Klutz and I were lounging on our patio, sipping martinis while the mockingbirds chattered and whistled in the huge oak tree next door. The blue sky, streaked in shades of orange, pink, and yellow, deepened into hues of coral and red as the sun began its descent behind the surrounding rooftops. Our dogs, Tess and Buddy, were sleeping by our feet. Occasionally one emitted a low growl as a fantasy rabbit scampered through its field of dreams.

The serenity of the moment was overpowering, and as I nodded off, wrapped in the arms of contentment, my martini glass slipped slowly from my grasp.

I was startled awake not so much by the sound of breaking glass but by Klutz who had jumped to his feet, knocking over his chair.

"I can't stand it anymore," he shouted. "It's too damn peaceful. No, it's too damn boring! We have got to do something—anything!!!"

I stared blankly at him. What the hell just happened?

Klutz, now pacing like a caged lion, asked, "Do you realize the most exciting thing that happens anymore is when the eye doctor pronounces our cataracts are 'ripe enough' for the government to pay for their removal?"

I tried to respond, but, ignoring me, he continued in a voice now dripping in sarcasm. "What about looking forward to the day when we can finally drive to Home Depot on a road that's not under construction? Oh, and let's not forget that Costco might be moving to our area. And maybe a Chick-fil-A! Now that's exciting!"

Klutz paused and took a deep breath, as if he is fortifying himself to launch into another tirade.

Amidst growing uncertainty, I asked, "Are you okay?"

"Of course, I'm okay," he replied emphatically. But he's not. His eyes were like slits in his lined, time-worn face. A hint of a smile touched the thin line of his mouth and then quickly vanished.

I cleaned up the broken glass and fixed myself another martini as I waited and wondered about Klutz. I didn't have to wait long because after a few moments he stopped circling the patio, sat down, and looked into my eyes.

"Diane," he said, his face softening. "I'm sorry. I know we moved to this community because of all the activities and to be around folks our age, but playing bumper cars with walkers and wheelchairs is not what I call fun. And neither is talking continuously about hemorrhoids, colonoscopies, over-peeing or under-peeing, and which doctor is best to fix any or all of them."

Popping an olive into his mouth, Klutz continued. "I'm tired of being old and acting old. I want to have another adventure before we can't anymore."

"That's it?" I asked as I rapidly closed my gaping mouth, letting out the breath that I didn't realize I was holding. "I thought you were going to tell me you had some disease and were dying. Or that one of our family had died! Or that you found another woman and were divorcing me."

I gulped the remnants of my martini as I attempted to collect my emotions. Meanwhile, Klutz remained silent, which was a good thing.

I waited for what seems like an eternity before asking, "So what do you have in mind?"

"I miss the water ... being on the water," Klutz replied.

I looked at him and, after another pause, asked, "Okay, like you want to take a cruise or an island vacation?"

I knew full well that this was not the adventure he was looking for, but I wasn't about to give in too easily.

Once again jumping to his feet, Klutz leaned over and whispered, "Let's go live on a boat. A really big boat. But not by ourselves. Let's get Jim and Cindy to join us. You know, like the four of us sharing a house. Only it's floating on the water."

After all this time together, I was not fazed one bit by any of Klutz's ideas. Instead, I simply made myself another martini and started writing a mental checklist for our next wild ride together.

Klutz resumed his brisk pacing. Except this time, it was not due to agitation. It was anticipation. Mid-stride, he wheeled around, grabbed his cell phone, and called our friends. Never mind that it was midnight. He was on a roll. And I was rolling right alone with him.

It took nearly a year to convince ourselves and Jim and Cindy that we could do this—buy and live 24/7 on a boat. Our friends thought we were crazy, and our families *knew* we were.

However, we were undeterred in our quest. And so onward we forged until at last we found our dream boat.

Our new home (or floating commune) is a Nordic 54 tug/trawler, classic in design and made for ocean cruising. She boasts two identical queen-sized quarters with attached facilities, a good-sized galley next to the salon, lots of windows, and two decks with a flybridge. There are also crew quarters, although rather small compared to the rest of the boat. From stem to stern, she is a queen of the high seas.

Her name?

Martini Alley III.

I know what you're thinking, but all of us like the name, and since "the third time's the charm ... "

Two years later, and we are still living our dream. With a real licensed boat captain at the helm, we've traveled from Cozumel to Cancún, around the Gulf Coast to the Florida Keys, and over to Bermuda and the Bahamas. We even cruised the Mississippi River up to the Great Lakes.

We endured minor storms and stayed out of the way of major ones. And Klutz, with the help of bulk supplies of Dramamine and the elixir of liquid courage, has survived our voyages without too many gastric mishaps.

Now we are once again back in Key West, enjoying the beautiful spectacle unfolding before us. The palm trees sway in the gentle breeze as the blazing sun begins its descent into the Gulf of Mexico.

"Here's to another perfect sunset," I say, raising my martini glass in tribute to the heavenly spectacle.

Klutz, Jim, and Cindy reply in unison, "*Salud*," as they clink their margarita and martini glasses to mine.

Always the consummate hostess, Cindy goes down to the galley to fix more drinks. "Snacks, anyone?" she asks as she passes the libations into our waiting hands.

Jim and Klutz respond simultaneously, "Of course!"

Putting the tray of appetizers on the table a few minutes later, Cindy starts to sit down when a gust of wind causes the boat to suddenly lurch starboard. She grabs the railing and steadies herself.

Klutz, also standing, is not as fortunate. His attempted rail-grabbing misses, and he tumbles over one of the deck chairs and crashes onto the deck.

Miraculously, he doesn't hurt himself.

Even more miraculously, he also doesn't spill a single drop of his martini!

The sun, now gone from sight, is replaced by a dazzling harvest moon. Stars so close you can almost touch them blanket the cloudless nighttime canopy of heaven.

Klutz drains his glass and then looks at each of us, a huge smile covering his face. "You know," he says, "It don't get no better'n this."

I look from my husband to our best buddies as a tsunami of disbelief washes over me.

Klutz and I were wrong.

For over fifty years we have been searching for our promised land. But, like the song, we'd been searching "in all the wrong places." Because our paradise isn't a place at all. It is simply *here* ...

... being with our friends...

... and together.

THE END

Or maybe not ...

Maybe we've just begun ...

Think about it. For many years, we have been seeking out new adventures on the water, near the water, in the water, and on dry land (with and without wheels).

But there is still a vast sky to explore. I read that there is a galaxy far-far-away called the Trappist-1 system with planets like Earth revolving around a star much like our sun. According to the article, the planet most similar to ours is named Kepler-4526.

Or even closer, in our own solar system, is Venus. Supposedly the atmosphere thirty to forty miles above the surface is hospitable for humans. It is not beyond imagination that some trillionaire will build a city above the clouds and need intrepid adventurers like the Klutzes to explore the used starship lots.

Maybe a space yacht is in our future?!?

Klutz's face lights up when I describe my findings. "Did you say spaceship? I've always wanted a spaceship. We could name it *Martini Alley IV!*"

He is almost giddy with the prospect of a space voyage as he sets off down the wormhole of spacecraft and extraterrestial travel.

This may be the beginning of a whole new quest, boldly going forth where no martini shaker has gone before ...

... to the Black Hole and beyond ...

and other swashbuckling adventures of a certified Klutz

Martini Alley

Steve Diane

ABOUT THE AUTHOR

Diane Klutz is a proud Vietnam veteran, nurse, wife, mother, grandmother, and author. Keeping to her credence that life is an ongoing adventure, she worked and studied her way through undergraduate and graduate school, post-graduate nurse practitioner certification, and finally earned her Ph.D. in nursing at the young age of fifty-nine.

During her forty-eight years in the medical profession, Diane worked in positions ranging from hospital staff nurse to clinical family nurse practitioner and in specialties ranging from acute care to public health.

As an assistant professor on the faculties at Midwestern State University in Wichita Falls, Texas Woman's University in Denton, and Texas A&M University in Corpus Christi, she also mentored undergraduate and graduate nursing students.

Diane's passion to write springs from a lifetime of reading and is based on her twofold beliefs that each person has a story just waiting to be told and that real life is frequently stranger than fiction.

Diane resides in Sun City, Texas, just north of Austin, with her husband of fifty years, her two cocker spaniels, and one cat.

When she is not writing, she enjoys gin martinis with two olives, reading, gardening, and playing shuffleboard with her friends at Wriggley's Pub.

Thank you for reading *Martini Alley and Other Swashbuckling Adventures of a Certified Klutz*. I hope you enjoyed it.

Want to stay updated with news about my books?
- like me on **facebook.com/dianeklutzauthor**
- visit my website: **dianeklutz.com**
- email me at: **diane@dianeklutz.com**

If you have a moment, please review *Martini Alley* at the store (or site) where you bought it. Reviews from readers like you are what sells books, and I would be so grateful for any words you might be willing to leave.

I hope we meet again between the pages of another book.

Diane

www.ingramcontent.com/pod-product-compliance
Lightning Source LLC
Chambersburg PA
CBHW050414120526
44590CB00015B/1964